NORTHUMBERLAND
FIRE & RESCUE SERVICE

NORTHUMBERLAND
FIRE & RESCUE SERVICE

RON HENDERSON

TEMPUS

To Ann and Caroline for their tolerance and patience during the many hours spent in compiling this history.

First published 2005

Tempus Publishing Limited
The Mill, Brimscombe Port,
Stroud, Gloucestershire, GL5 2QG
www.tempus-publishing.com

© Ron Henderson, 2005

British Library Cataloguing in Publication Data.
A catalogue record for this book is available from the British Library.

ISBN 0 7524 3540 X

Typesetting and origination by Tempus Publishing Limited.
Printed in Great Britain.

CONTENTS

ACKNOWLEDGEMENTS

A history of this type cannot be completed easily without the help of others. It would be remiss not to mention the help and support given by the following people. First of all, thanks to Chief Fire Officer John McCall for his unceasing support with the project, and to his successor Brian Hesler. Similar gratitude is accorded to Sub Officer Adrian Slasser for his hospitality, trust and support and for making the brigade's photographic collection available, the majority of which are used to illustrate this history, together with the author's own collection. Thank you to the following individuals who kindly made their personal photographic collection open for perusal and use, or helped in other ways: Ian Moore and Trevor Welham for access to their comprehensive photographic archives; Dennis Barker; Ronnie Black; Angus Patterson; Michael Wood; R. Wright, NCFRS; Ruth Bissell for her clerical support. The following organisations were very helpful: Berwick Photo Centre; Bailiff Museum, Alnwick; Fire International; Ray Marshall and the library staff, *Newcastle Chronicle & Journal*, Tyne and Wear Libraries; Northumberland County Records Office; and any other individuals and organisations whose name has been inadvertently omitted. Last but not least, thanks to all the firefighters and personnel of Northumberland for their hospitality and encouragement over the past fifty years.

INTRODUCTION

The most northerly county of England is Northumberland. Covering an area of almost 2,000 square miles, it is one of the largest but least densely populated counties, with apparently five times more sheep than people. As with all Britain's counties, the population of Northumberland is dependent on the efficiency and professionalism of the county council's servants for ensuring the quality of life and the well-being of its residents and visitors. This history looks at one of the noblest of organisations, the fire brigade.

This history begins with the formation of Northumberland County Fire Brigade in 1948 and documents the efforts to attain continuity and progress in the face of postwar austerity measures. From this period on, it describes the appliances, premises and activities of the organisation and some of the many people responsible for the fire brigade's development and professionalism. The local government boundary changes in 1974 caused the county to become smaller, when the southern Northumberland towns were transferred to the new county of Tyne and Wear. Despite these changes, the remainder of the county continues to maintain its own fire brigade, unlike its associated police and ambulance services, which have merged with neighbouring authorities. With further mergers being planned as a result of the government's Fire Service Modernisation Plan, it is hoped that this fifty-year history will serve as a lasting tribute to all those people, both male and female, that have all contributed to making the Northumberland Fire & Rescue Service one of the most professional, capable, courteous and contented brigades in the country.

CHAPTER 1

IN THE BEGINNING

The origins of Northumberland Fire & Rescue Service can be traced back to 1948 when new county, county borough councils and associated fire authorities were formed. The brigade's roots, though, can be traced back much further, and many of the original fixtures and fittings of the newly formed Northumberland County Fire Brigade were inherited from former urban district and rural district fire brigades. Most of the big towns in Northumberland had formed professional fire brigades by the turn of the twentieth century, particularly at Blyth, Gosforth, Newburn, Wallsend and Whitley Bay, which all employed full-time firemen. The other urban and rural district councils had part-time fire brigades mostly equipped with trailer pumps towed by council lorries or any other kind of vehicle that was available. In some cases councils appointed neighbouring fire brigades to provide fire cover, such as Ashington Urban and Rural District areas, where the Northumberland and Durham Collieries Fire & Rescue Brigade was appointed to provide fire cover.

In 1939 war was declared again and in view of likely increases in aerial bombing attacks it was decided in 1941 to place all the nation's fire brigades under single control, the Home Office, resulting in the formation of the National Fire Service. For the first time, there was a unified rank and pay structure and a large degree of standardisation of equipment. Naturally, many councils were against this process but were reassured that following the cessation of hostilities the fire brigade would be returned to local authority control. War ended in 1945 and the fire brigades were indeed returned to local authority control, but in not quite the same way as in prewar days. Under the Fire Services Act 1947 the county council became the fire authority for the whole of the administrative county of Northumberland. Instead of individual urban and rural district fire brigades, the services were all placed under county council control. From 1 April 1948, Northumberland County Fire Brigade became the main provider of fire brigades in the county. This Act did not pose too many problems for the large city and county borough fire brigades that already had centralised headquarters, premises and so on, but for rural areas – Northumberland being no exception – the brigade had to start from virtually nothing. First of all a chief fire officer had to be appointed, and then a suitable headquarters and control needed to be found, as well as other resources such as centralised workshop facilities.

Following the disbanding of the National Fire Service, there were many surplus fire officers seeking the many appointments created within the proposed new fire authorities. To make things easier for those responsible for making the appointments, a book was published and distributed to all parties concerned, listing and describing the careers of all those persons eligible for the appointments. Northumberland's focus was narrowed on one William Bell Muir, a Scotsman by birth, who came with a first-class *curriculum vitae*. At forty-five years of age, he had already

Chief Fire Officer William Bell Muir (right) (in office 1948–1969).

reached the heights of fire force commander and firemaster designate of the county of Fife in Scotland. After leaving the Royal Air Force in 1929 he enrolled in the City of Perth Fire Brigade and within seven years had risen to the position of firemaster of the City of Dunfermline Fire Brigade. He had an impressive list of qualifications and commendations, including the MBE for gallantry and leadership during the Clydebank Blitz; he received the OBE in the 1946 New Year's Honours List. Having also been awarded a commendation for the Clydebank Blitz fires of 1941, he later gained fame and further commendations for his actions at the Burngrange shale pit disaster on 10 January 1944. Fifteen miners lost their lives in an underground fire here, and this incident was the first of its type at which firemen had entered underground mine workings to save life and extinguish fire. William Muir was successful with his application and commenced his long tenure as chief fire officer of Northumberland on 15 March 1948. His deputy chief officer was a former Liverpool Police Fire Brigade officer by the name of George Leslie Taylor, aged thirty-five.

Other senior officer appointments were: R. Noble, officer in charge, South Sub-Area; J.H. Taylor, officer in charge, North Sub-Area; J.H. Crossly, water and communications officer (these three were all former Newcastle City fire officers); J.B. Harkins, transport officer; F. Rushbrook, fire prevention and photography officer (both from Edinburgh); and H. Cooper, mobilising officer (ex-South Shields Fire Brigade).

Then there were eight firewomen employed for control-room duties and of course the civilian posts comprising clerks, typists, cooks and stores officers etc. The complement of full-time personnel was determined by the Fire Services (Transfer of Persons) Regulations 1948, under which it was mandated that 'all full-time firemen serving within the area of the County Fire Brigade and who were not successful in obtaining an appointment above the rank of fireman be

Chief Fire Officer Muir and the original headquarters staff outside Roseworth East in 1948.

automatically transferred on 1 April 1948 to the County Fire Brigade in the rank of fireman'. The initial establishment also made provisions for a complement of fifty-eight temporary full-time firemen to be employed until the ultimate establishment was reached. These people were former National Fire Service personnel who enlisted during the war and were theoretically due to be returned to the general civilian workforce; suitable applicants were now invited to apply for the temporary posts on three-month contracts. On the expiry of these contracts, it was found that the firemen were still required, so the contracts were extended for a further three months, taking them up to 31 October. The duty periods at the time were sixty hours each week at Blyth, Gosforth, Hexham, Newburn, Wallsend and Whitley Bay, while the men at Alnwick, Berwick and Morpeth worked eighty-hour weeks consisting of forty-eight hours on duty and forty-eight hours off.

The contracts of the temporary firemen were again extended, this time for a further six months, prompting concern from the Fire Brigades Union regarding the uncertainty of these people's future. The union urged that as many of these men as possible should be engaged on permanent contracts in preference to filling the vacancies with new recruits. New stipulations had just been agreed, though not yet implemented, regarding the necessary physical attributes of firemen, such as chest expansion and height, together with a maximum age limit. While some of the temporary firemen clearly did not conform to these new criteria, there were no reasons why the men should not be given permanent employment. It was decided that while the age limit was to be strictly adhered to, some tolerance was allowed on the other criteria, and those temporary firemen who considered themselves otherwise qualified were allowed to apply for permanent employment. Under this agreement, nine of the men were immediately employed on permanent contracts.

The question of training future recruits was considered in the brigade's first years of existence and it was decided that it would not be practical to establish a training school in Northumberland. Durham County Fire Brigade, however, decided to set up a training centre at their Felling on Tyne fire station with a capacity for twenty men, and offered to undertake the training of Northumberland's recruits at the centre. The first four recruits were dispatched to Felling on 1 November and at the end of the course two qualified with distinction and were judged the best and second-best recruits, while the other two achieved third and eighth positions. Fireman Dingwall from Wallsend was awarded the presentation silver axe as the most outstanding trainee.

The transition from the National Fire Service to county control was completed smoothly and one of the new chief fire officer's first public appearances was at the headquarters of the London Fire Brigade at the invitation of the Secretary of State to mark the transfer of fire brigades to county and county borough councils. Back home in Northumberland, an 'Order of the Day' issued to the chief fire officer and the brigade on 1 April by the chairman of the county council, Alderman William Smith, included the following injunction: 'I expect yours to become one of the most capable, courteous and contented brigades in the country.' This history will hopefully prove that the expectation was fulfilled.

The brigade used as its headquarters the premises which had formerly been used by the regional headquarters of the No.1 Region of the National Fire Service, which was transferred to the county council's ownership. This consisted of three large houses at The Grove, Gosforth. Roseworth East contained the actual headquarters and brigade control room, Roseworth West became the residence of the chief fire officer, and No.33 The Grove, on the opposite side to the

Chief Fire Officer Muir and Mrs Muir on the doorstep of their spacious residence at Roseworth West, The Grove, Gosforth, in June 1948.

Roseworth houses, was acquired temporarily, to be handed back to the urban district council as soon as possible. In the grounds of Roseworth East, a large prefabricated hut, together with a brick Air Raid Precautions control room, was adapted for use as a brigade store and mess room. The premises were in a state of disrepair due to lack of maintenance during the war, but thanks to the efforts of the brigade's personnel, a good cleaning and redecoration soon made the premises habitable. The use of firemen for these duties effected a considerable saving in labour costs.

The brigade's original fire stations were located as follows: Allendale, Golden Lion Hotel; Alnwick, Clayport; Amble, Queen Street; Belford, West Street; Bellingham, Foundary Yard; Berwick, Wallace Street; Blyth, Union Street, with six houses at Oxford Street and Princess Louise Road; Gosforth, High Street, plus one house at Rothwell Road; Haltwhistle, Rosevean, with flat above and accommodation at Hawthorne House; Haydon Bridge, John Martin Street; Hexham, West Orchard House; Morpeth, Newgate Street; Newburn, High Street, with flat above; Prudhoe, Council Yard; Rothbury, Bridge Street; Seahouses, Bamburgh Castle Hotel; Wallsend, Lawson Street, with nine firemen's houses at Coach Road; Whitley Bay, York Road, plus five flats above and Victoria Garage; Wooler, Cheviot Street.

The fire stations, none of which were deemed to be entirely suitable, fell into two categories distributed between two divisions: North Division, with headquarters at Alnwick, and South Division, with headquarters at Gosforth. The categories were those that were built as fire stations before the war but were now rendered inadequate because of changed circumstances, improved conditions of service and the standards of cover, and those that were purely temporary premises erected to meet the emergency needs of the war. In many instances it was suggested that the pre-war stations posed significant handicaps, notably at Gosforth, where the proximity of the Council Chambers confined drill periods to times outside normal office hours or when meetings were not being held. In addition to this, the station housed the town's mortuary on the ground floor, a facility that remained there for several more years. Wallsend also had its problems

The North Division's headquarters and fire station at Clayport, Alnwick, in 1948. This was the first of the county's full-time fire stations to be replaced.

The brigade photographer was tasked with photographing the personnel at each of the brigade's fire stations. This is Gosforth's establishment in July 1948. Company Officer William Sewell is in the centre with Section Leader Jack Stephenson to his right. The uniforms still bear NFS insignia.

as drills and normal routine operations had to be suspended when the neighbouring court was in session. Furthermore, it was identified that the appliance accommodation was insufficient to house the minimum number of fire appliances that was currently required to meet the prescribed standards of fire cover. Wallsend was mentioned again, as one of its appliances had to be housed in premises belonging to the borough council. At Whitley Bay, early negotiations with F.W. Woolworth & Co. and the urban district council were successful in acquiring land at the rear of the fire station to enable the site to be extended by 326 square yards. Extensive alterations were required, but were not immediately approved on the grounds of economy. The entire building and the residential quarters in particular were threatened by damp, and the plumbing system, installed in the previous century, was understandably not reliable. Of the stations erected during the war, most consisted of prefabricated buildings dating from 1941, which had now reached the end of their useful life. There were some stations that were set up on requisitioned land as a temporary measure, some of which were in a condemned state such as the one at Haltwhistle. Some stations were described as being 'derelict'. At Allendale, the station needed structural alterations to provide additional height for the accommodation of a towing vehicle. Hexham's fire station consisted of a two-storey house together with a five-bay garage that was erected by the National Fire Service. In 1946 the property was purchased by the British Red Cross Society, which was permitted by the NFS to have possession of the whole of the house with the exception of the ground floor, which was used by the fire brigade as living quarters. This arrangement was the source of continual uncertainty in the ensuing years. Very ambitiously it was proposed in principle that all of the brigade's premises, including the headquarters, should be gradually replaced by new buildings. These ambitious plans prompted the chairman of the fire brigades committee, the chief fire officer and the brigade's fire prevention officer to visit Fife in Scotland, where there were three fire stations of a type suitable for Northumberland, on which it was hoped to base the design of the brigade's future stations. As a starting point it was planned, subject to Home Office approval, to erect five new two-bay stations, or alternatively, one three-bay and four two-bay stations, in the years up to 1954.

At the inception of the brigade, Wallsend, Gosforth, Newburn, Whitley Bay, Blyth, Alnwick and Berwick operated full-time appliances, supervised by a station officer. The remainder were retained stations, although Morpeth and Hexham attained full-time status within a few months. With the exception of Wallsend, all of the full-time stations also had a complement of retained firemen. The full-time establishment, up to and including sub officers, totalled fifty-five men and there were seven vacancies. Initial recruitment to fill the vacancies proved difficult, as the brigade was only interested in recruiting tradesmen, but eventually four suitable applicants were employed: a plumber, a coach painter, a fitter and a mechanic.

Establishments, both structural and in terms of personnel, were agreed by the Home Office in accordance with risk categories in each brigade area. In Northumberland's case, the allocation of appliances was set at fifty vehicles and forty-five pumps. This total included nine former local authority machines, with the remainder being former National Fire Service allocations, which were vehicles based on Austin, Bedford and Fordson chassis, together with an assortment of trailer pumps. From a preliminary survey it was identified that the brigade was faced with an intensive programme of overhauling, refitting and in some instances redesigning of some of these appliances, although in the chief fire officer's opinion, the county council did possess a comprehensive selection of appliances which in number, type and quality at least equalled that likely to be held by any other comparable brigade. As well as the appliances, the brigade was issued with eight former NFS staff cars.

The appliances consisted of:

FULL TIME
Major pumps   6
Pump escape   4
Water tenders   1

RETAINED
Major pumps   2
Light pumps   6
Water tenders   2

The retained stations were mostly equipped with wartime towing vehicles, which were simply Austin vans with seats for personnel in the rear, and facilities for towing a trailer pump. In order to increase the usefulness of these vans, conversion kits were supplied by the Home Office, which equipped the vehicles with a water tank and hose reel and pump. Also transferred were three emergency tenders, two of them former UDC vehicles and one a Home Office issue. None of them were manned in the post-war era as there was no establishment for this type of appliance, although the brigade would return to the idea of emergency tenders in the ensuing years. In addition, there was one major pump available from the National Coal Board at Ashington. The previously agreed contractual obligations with regard to the provision of fire cover in the Ashington area and surrounding districts was a major issue at the inception of the county brigade, because of the drawback that calls to colliery premises would always have first priority. In that event, the county brigade would have to mobilise other resources in order to

A typical Northumberland Austin auxiliary towing vehicle and Coventry Climax trailer pump of kinds that were prevalent throughout the brigade's retained stations. Note the convenient support for the suction hose.

deal with fires within the Ashington district when the Coal Board's engine was engaged at colliery incidents. In fact, it was deemed that these occasions would prove to be comparatively rare and, in the past, the Coal Board had provided a satisfactory service. Leaving aside the capital expenditure involved in the acquisition of suitable premises, fire appliances and equipment, the annual costs of maintaining a comparable county-run fire brigade service was estimated to be four times greater than that which the Coal Board was charging, and therefore in those circumstances, and given that no suitable sites or premises were available in the district, the agreement with the Coal Board remained.

So bureaucratic were the early Home Office establishment rulings that permission had to be sought just to increase the establishment by one wheelbarrow pump. Such a request made 1948 was for one of these pumps for the local fire party at Holy Island, as a substitute for three manually operated pumps on the island. Before being issued, however, the clerk of Norham and Islandshires Rural District Council was asked for an assurance that the following four conditions would be observed:

1 that suitable accommodation be provided to house the appliance
2 that an organised fire party of not less than three operatives be in existence
3 that it be clearly understood that persons operating the appliance did so at their own risk
4 that every outbreak of fire be reported to the brigade.

The matter was referred to Holy Island Parish Council, which was not prepared to accept these terms and conditions and declined the offer of the pump, which was then assigned to Berwick. There were also three local fire units at Ford Castle (near Berwick), Alnmouth and Hauxley. The Alnmouth and Ford Castle units were equipped with a light motorised trailer pump, and Hauxley with three manual

This type of Morris-Sigmund trailer pump, manufactured on the Team Valley Trading Estate at Gateshead, was towed behind the water tenders. A similar unit was mounted on the appliance. This example was still in service when pictured at Whitley Bay in 1970.

pumps. The Ford Castle pump was replaced in 1950 by a manual pump because the water supply was insufficient to feed a motor pump and because of the difficulties found in maintaining a trained crew. Alnmouth's trailer pump was withdrawn at the same time because the area could be covered adequately by Alnwick Fire Station, and all of the Hauxley manuals were removed because there was no organised fire party to maintain and operate them. The original allocation was made here because of inadequate telephone facilities at Hauxley and Radcliffe.

On the subject of vehicles, it was recognised that the setting up of a suitable workshop was a matter of urgency because of the specialist nature of fire appliances. It was suggested that specialist technical and experienced supervision of maintenance could only really be given by an internal organisation. There was no suitable accommodation attached to any fire stations, but adjacent to Gosforth's fire station, on the Royalty Cinema car-park site, was a large garage built by the NFS, which had been used rent-free by prior agreement. This site appeared to be an ideal temporary solution and negotiations were immediately begun to secure the site on a short-term tenancy until more suitable accommodation became available. In the meantime, the Home Office workshops at Stanley Road, Leeds, were made available for urgent repairs. Also, a small and by no means adequate repair organisation was set up at No.33 The Grove, manned by certain tradesmen taken from firefighting strength. It was proposed that as soon as a suitable transport workshop was acquired, Home Office sanction would be sought to authorise the employment of an additional ten staff for the workshops. Authorisation was duly granted with the proviso that the ten men, including one sub officer or workshops officer, would be liable for firefighting duties as well. Ten tradesmen were duly appointed, and in accordance with the Home Office's wishes, they were tasked with manning the second appliance at Gosforth during weekdays, a duty that lasted for almost twenty years. Retained personnel drawn from the local council's workforce manned the appliances at night times and weekends.

This historic June 1948 view shows the original workshop at The Grove, Gosforth. On the left, a wartime Fordson staff car is being worked on and at the rear is the brigade's sole Fordson WOT6 water tender.

This impressive Dennis Big 4 pump escape at Wallsend was delivered to the borough's fire brigade in 1934. The helmets of the crew show that the picture was taken in the early 1950s.

Many of the inherited appliances needed a complete repaint, as, apart from the former urban district appliances, the NFS vehicles were still attired in their emergency wartime grey livery. There were forty-one fire engines and thirty-three trailer pumps to repaint. Some were repainted in the traditional red colour by fire station staff and the others were either repainted commercially by a Newcastle firm or by workshop personnel. Negotiations to secure the large garage situated in the Royalty Cinema car park for use as a workshop were successful, and an initial tenancy agreement for twelve months from 1 August 1948 was signed. Thereafter it was renewable quarterly. This was not a very sound proposition but nevertheless it gave the brigade some welcome breathing space.

At the close of the first year Muir and his team had established the brigade's headquarters, established both uniformed and civilian staff and set up a centralised workshop. This was enough to be getting on with, but many more improvements and adjustments would follow in the ensuing years.

The incidence of fires during the new brigade's first month was small and largely confined to seasonal outbreaks of grass, heath and haystack fires. The only noteworthy outbreak involved the steamship *Archgrove*, moored at Cowpen Staithes, North Blyth. The appliances and personnel used in the extinguishing of this fire had to be ferried across the river. By the end of the year the number of fires for the entire county was still relatively small: there had been 521 emergency calls and 351 actual fires. There were 73 chimney fires and 40 false alarms. Calls to other areas totalled 45, and 12 emergency special service calls were dealt with. The busiest stations in the brigade at this time were Wallsend, with a total of 86 calls, and Gosforth, with 79. However, Wallsend did not stay top of the league for long. Incidents of note included the brigade's first emergency special service call, which was to rescue a youth who had fallen down the hold of a derelict ship that was beached at Cullercoats. During August the brigade was inundated with calls when exceptionally heavy rains in the northern parts of the county resulted in heavy flooding. From 2.30 p.m. on the 12th, twenty-one separate calls were dealt with, and at Berwick the normal resources of the brigade were augmented by a rowing boat, the property of the retained station officer, which, mounted upon a lorry, provided a mobile means of rescue for families marooned by the floodwaters. In all, eleven people and their effects were rescued by this method. In addition to calls of an emergency and humanitarian nature, the resources of the brigade were deployed in pumping out flooded open-cast coal sites at Goswick, Broomhill, Dinnington, Plessey and Whitley Bay, which in total involved almost 760 man hours. The mayor of Berwick, on behalf of the citizens of the borough, later expressed his appreciation of the good

Firemen from Belford tackle a haystack fire at Easington Demesne in December 1949. Note that two of the firemen are still wearing wartime metal 'soup plate' helmets.

The New Deleval Co-operative Society's bakeries at Newsham, Blyth, the morning after the devastating fire.

work done by units of the County Fire Brigade during the recent floods. On 21 August fire severely damaged the New Deleval Co-operative Society's bakeries' premises at Newsham, Blyth. Exploding oil-fired ovens caused a fire that destroyed a large part of the building. Appliances from Blyth, Whitley Bay, Morpeth and Gosforth attended the blaze. Damage was estimated at £34,000, making this fire the largest individual loss since the brigade's inception.

It was noted very early on in the brigade's development that the western area of the county could suffer from water shortages in cases of fire in the large tracts of forestry and moorland, and an appeal for the supply of six water tenders carrying at least 400 gallons of water was made to the Home Office to alleviate this problem. Muir developed a particular interest in the techniques of firefighting on Forestry Commission land and participated in many exercises and meetings regarding these risks. It also prompted him to undertake hours of research and invention in developing new techniques for protecting and extinguishing fires in the Kielder, Redesdale and Kyloe Forest regions. Another problem that became a matter of concern was the remoteness of fires in these areas and the considerable distances between the fire and the nearest telephone. The terrain frequently could not be traversed by vehicles, which meant that communication had to be maintained by runners. To counter these difficulties, it was recommended that four portable 'walkie talkie' wireless sets be acquired, subject of course to Home Office approval.

As the second year of the new brigade progressed, Berwick was at the receiving end of another commendation, when the chief fire officer expressed his thanks to Fireman O.F. Miller, who, on 1 March, played a principal part in the rescue of two boys who had been cut off by the rising tide while playing in an alcove in the sea wall. After descending 30ft down a wall, Miller attached a safety line to each of the boys who in turn were hauled up by the remaining members of the crew.

The commendation stated that 'although throughout the operation Fireman Miller was constantly buffeted by heavy seas and while utilising the lifeline for the rescue relied himself upon a utility rope, he displayed not only considerable skill but also a cool disregard for his own safety'.

Since the brigade's inception, mutual aid schemes had been drawn up between neighbouring brigades whereby assistance to and from these brigades would be available in cases of emergency. These brigades were Newcastle & Gateshead Joint Fire Service, Durham County Fire Brigade, Tynemouth Borough Fire Brigade and South Eastern Fire Brigade, Scotland. A scheme with Cumberland Fire Brigade was established the following year. An additional financial arrangement with Newcastle & Gateshead Joint Fire Service was agreed, after much negotiation between the Home Secretary and the Tyne Improvement Commission, regarding the use of Newcastle's Walker-based fireboat for the protection of the properties alongside the river in Wallsend. The terms were that Northumberland would pay one third of the operating costs of the vessel. This figure was substantially reduced later when the Home Office gave the Newcastle Brigade a 75 per cent grant towards the costs. This arrangement lasted until the boat was withdrawn as being beyond economical repair in 1958. The South Shields Fire Brigade also operated a fireboat and negotiations were started with that authority regarding the use of the vessel for Northumberland's land bordering the River Tyne.

In late April 1949 four operational pumps and a service van and pump manned by workshop crews under the command of the transport officer J.B. Harkins were deployed on the long journey to West Hartlepool, where a disastrous fire destroyed thousands of timber pit props on a 57-acre storage site. The blaze started at 8.37 p.m. on 27 April and over forty pumps were

The first fatal accident attended by the brigade occurred in March 1949, when this lorry load of petrol cans caught fire at Dinnington near Newcastle Airport.

A Northumberland crew with trailer pump at the West Hartlepool timber yard fire.

eventually ordered to the fire. Thirty-three main jets were put into operation before the fire was brought under control, by which time 250,000 standards of timber and thirty-eight railway wagons had been destroyed. Two thirds of the pit props were saved from the conflagration and the workshop crew earned high praise from the chief fire officer of Durham for their efforts when a number of pumps which had broken down in the course of the fire were brought back into commission. This feat of distance has not been beaten since in relation to an actual fire, although a special service call of grander proportions would later see the brigade travel even further afield. It was the Hartlepool fire that prompted northern region fire brigades to establish mutual aid schemes.

The last bastion of manually operated street fire alarm points in the county was at Blyth, and in August 1949 this seven-point system was finally discontinued. Inherited by the county in 1948, the system saw little use as the town's citizens preferred to use police 'pillar' telephones.

Wartime steel 'soup plate' helmets were still being worn by the firemen, but at the latter end of 1949 the brigade examined various types of helmet in order to determine what would be the standard issue for the firemen. A plastic 'Brighton' pattern helmet from the Glasgow firm of Hendry was selected and 434 helmets were promptly ordered. Officers were equipped with more luxurious 'Cromwell' types.

1949 had been a busy one for the brigade. There was an unusually large number of fires caused by an exceptionally dry summer, and on several occasions during the year it had been necessary to deploy the whole of the brigade's resources to attend incidents. The locations and outbreaks of most of these fires and the fact that the peak occurred at weekends suggested that they followed a train of weekend visitors from towns in the south and eastern parts of the county. Of the total number of calls, 761 of them were actual fires and 136 were for chimney fires. There were 127

A lone fireman prepares foam equipment at a road accident on the Great North Road in February 1949. Road accidents would later become an increasingly common scenario for the county's firefighters.

turnouts to other brigade's areas. Top of the list this time was Gosforth, Wallsend moving down to second place. Gosforth Fire Brigade remained the busiest station throughout the remainder of the county brigade's original existence. The station's turn-out area and population, and its close proximity to the City of Newcastle, ensured this.

At the government's instigation, following the implementation of the Civil Defence (Fire Service) Regulations 1949, it was ordered that every fire authority must recruit an auxiliary organisation known as the Auxiliary Fire Service (AFS). The provisional requirement was for two male auxiliaries for each full-time member, one for every part-time member plus 10 per cent of that number of auxiliary females. In Northumberland's case this meant that some 600 auxiliaries would have to be recruited. The organisation was manned on an unpaid, voluntary basis using, in the first instance, former NFS standard fire appliances issued on loan from the Home Office. Members usually met at selected fire stations on one evening each week and on weekends, taking part in joint exercises with neighbouring fire brigades. Despite measures to encourage every prospective enquirer, the brigade had managed to enrol only thirteen recruits during the first campaign. More intensive recruiting methods followed to try and swell the numbers. By August thirty-three applications for enrolment in the AFS had been received and twenty-eight, including five females, had been accepted. The brigade was concerned at the slow rate of recruitment and consequently set up a Mobile Recruiting Unit using its own resources to assist with a three-day recruiting campaign held in main centres of population in the county. Of a total of 151 recruits accepted during the campaign, the enrolment of forty males and thirty-eight females were directly attributed to the activities of the Mobile Recruiting Unit. Arrangements were also made with the Illuminations Committee at Whitley Bay for an illuminated set piece to be exhibited there as part of the town's illuminations. All of this was a preliminary to an intense national campaign sponsored by the Home Office, to be held in October. Northumberland's AFS section was initially allocated, on loan from the Home Office, four large Coventry Climax trailer pumps and three light Morris Sigmund pumps for deployment throughout the brigade, where it was hoped that circumstances would permit a nucleus of an AFS organisation to be recruited and trained. As there was nothing available to tow the trailer pumps, a request was made to the Home Office for the issue of three Austin towing vehicles, together with one self-propelled pump. These were stopgap measures until the Home Office embarked on a massive new appliance-building programme.

Up to 1950 the brigade's staff cars, used by the officers, consisted of wartime requisitioned vehicles or Home Office allocations, but in February, following recent county council approval, the first of two Austin A40 saloon cars was delivered, finished in the standard black livery of the day. A follow-up order for three Vauxhall Wyvern cars for delivery during the following year was changed to Austin A40s as they were a cheaper option and enabled greater standardisation. The question of new fire appliances came under discussion at this time and, with the brigade keen to update the fleet, one of the first six water tenders ordered by and supplied to the Home Office from James Whitson and Sons Ltd of West Drayton, Middlesex, was allocated to Northumberland. Water tenders produced by other private firms were also investigated and one additional machine, incorporating specific modifications designed to meet the special requirements of the county, was also ordered. This example was constructed by Messrs Carmichael & Sons of Worcester, who were also making appliances under Home Office contract. It had previously been determined that the brigade's requirements for the 1950–51 financial year were unlikely to exceed the purchase of three water tenders, and after the orders for the above two appliances were placed, notification was received regarding another manufacturer that was marketing water tenders on the same type of Commer chassis. This was the firm of Alfred Miles Ltd, of Cheltenham,

The first staff cars bought by the County Brigade were Austin A40 types. One of the first, ETY140, is pictured here at The Grove in 1951.

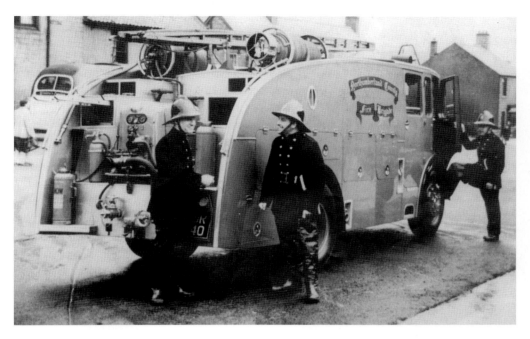

Alnwick's firemen proudly show off their brand new Commer-Whitson water tender, the county's first new fire engine. The appliance was in service for over twenty years. (Courtesy of Bailiff Museum, Alnwick)

Gloucestershire. Their model incorporated several improvements, the most important of which was the use of aluminium alloy in the construction of the bodywork. Consequently an order was placed for a Miles water tender on a Commer chassis, making a total of three new appliances. The delivery of the Miles appliance would be significant as far as the future fire appliance fleet went. An offer of small wheelbarrow pumps from the Home Office was also considered and, since the chance of acquiring such pumps from other sources at a reasonable price was low, a total of six were promptly purchased. The lack of small-capacity pumps had been severely felt during the 1949 drought and it was envisaged that there would be a use for these small pumps for salvage work and special service calls. These small pumps, configured in a wheelbarrow type of framework, usually sat in the appliance room where they could be readily manhandled into the cab of an appliance or into the back of the station's utility van.

Station Officer C.G. Fawkes, one of two such officers on the establishment at Wallsend, was successful this year in obtaining an overseas position with the Anglo-Iranian Oil Company, and was replaced by a transferred officer from the London Fire Brigade. Taking up position on 27 January, within a week the new station officer applied to be transferred back to London for domestic reasons and duly returned south. He was replaced by J. Garside from Nottingham City, who later went on to attain the rank of chief fire officer.

Ten new recruits passed out from the training school during the early part of the year, one of them with distinction and the award of the silver axe for being the best recruit on the course. This was the second occasion that a Northumberland Brigade member had won this prestigious award. This time Fireman K. Shell of Morpeth was the recipient. Despite ongoing problems with the temporary firemen, recruitment from outside still went on and at the beginning of 1950 119 applications had been received of which twenty were eventually accepted. Recruitment for retained staff was continuous, in an effort to maintain a balance between appointments and resignations. The method for calling out the retained personnel was by air-raid sirens mounted on towers at fire stations or other prominent buildings. However, the war was still fresh in people's minds and the sound of the air-raid sirens wailing again was a continual cause of consternation. The possibility of modifying the warning sounds was investigated in 1950 and of the several manufacturers that were approached one was found that claimed to have produced a device which cut out the rising and falling note of the siren. Problems with the types of sirens used at the brigade's twenty-one sites prevented the idea from being pursued. The chief fire officer was asked by the Fire Brigades Committee to continue to pursue investigations into the possibility of alternative methods of calling out the retained section of the brigade. An alternative method was indeed found, but it took twenty years of technological developments before the sirens finally sounded their last mournful wails.

Newcastle appliances, seen in the background, have been called in to assist the Gosforth brigade at a Home Office Inspectorate exercise at Moor Court Flats, Gosforth in 1950. Inspector Percy Booth is on the right taking notes.

CHAPTER 2

PREMISES

The suitability of Northumberland's fire stations was a continuing problem for many reasons. Apart from the prewar fire stations, many of the other buildings were built on land or utilised premises that were requisitioned during the war, suitable rental agreements or compensation payments being made to the former owners. The former requisition agreements were due to end in December 1952 and if the owners did not wish to continue with the existing agreements or negotiate new terms then the fire brigade would be made homeless.

Two years into the brigade's existence the situation was as follows:

The station at Alnwick was identified as being in a particularly precarious position. This station, the Northern Sub-Area Headquarters, was held on an annual tenancy basis from Alnwick Urban District Council and was on a site that was urgently required by the council for

The county's sole Fordson WOT6 four-wheel-drive water tender came to grief in October 1951 when it ran off the road whilst en route to a tractor fire. At the time it was operating from Alnwick.

housing purposes. This fact and the steadily deteriorating condition of the building were making replacement an increasingly urgent matter. A suitable alternative site was identified on the west side of the Great North Road and subject to planning clearances negotiations were begun for the acquisition of this site.

The station at Newburn was badly sited in relation to the fire risk in the area. Its distance from the main residential areas made the recruitment of retained firemen for the second appliance a continual problem. The officer in charge lived in a house above the appliance room and the firemen were accommodated in a hut at the rear of the station.

A replacement for Bellingham's station was also becoming imperative. This site was a temporary one and was said to be in a very poor state of repair. Unfortunately postwar shortages prevented the Secretary of State from giving approval to release expenditure for new fire station buildings and he suggested the alternative of securing other premises that could be adapted for fire brigade purposes. As a stopgap, an approach was made to the owners of the recently vacated Reeds Charity School to secure the premises for the housing of the town's fire engine. This did not come to fruition so the landowner of the present fire station site, the Duke of Northumberland, was approached through his agent with a view to buying the site together with some adjoining land. It was found that this was not possible but an alternative site of three-quarters of an acre was made available and negotiations immediately started to secure the land. In the meantime, in view of the state of the current premises, a new prefabricated hut was erected on the site.

Things were not too good at Hexham either. The lack of a suitable central fire station in this area proved to be a big handicap to training and development, since the four retained stations at Allendale, Bellingham, Haltwhistle and Haydon Bridge had no training facilities. Hexham's fire station was originally acquired on requisition by the NFS in 1942 and was later sold by the original owners to the British Red Cross Society, who in 1946 were allowed by arrangement with the NFS to occupy the upper floor, with the fire personnel on the ground floor. The appliances were housed in a separate garage next to the house, which was built, together with a hose-drying tower and petrol store, by the NFS. The situation changed in 1950 when the British Red Cross Society intimated that they wished to occupy further parts of the building. Upon being pressed to sell the property to the council, the society flatly refused, on the grounds that not only was the house needed badly but also that its loss would be a serious blow to the organisation's many members and voluntary helpers. The council felt bound to accede to the society's wishes and conceded that they could make a strong claim to the property. On the basis that the property would become wholly owned by the British Red Cross Society at the end of 1952, and in the event that no other suitable property could be found in that time, the only satisfactory solution was to build a new fire station on a new site.

At Haltwhistle the premises consisted of a garage erected on requisitioned land together with a condemned cottage, which was held on a quarterly tenancy. It was unlikely that the owners would agree to new terms and, as the premises were totally inadequate, early replacement was necessary here also.

At Belford the station was part of an old school that had been requisitioned in 1944. The means of access was totally unsatisfactory. Besides, the station was prone to flooding and indeed was flooded to a depth of 4ft on one occasion. During some severe floods in August 1948, a small bridge providing egress from the station was washed away and an alternative way out had to be made at the rear of the station by partially dismantling a boundary wall to give access to the roadway. To prevent a recurrence, the county architect was asked to prepare an estimate for the reinstatement of the wall and the provision of gates. It was felt that the gates could be made more cheaply by fire brigade personnel; eventually approval was given for the necessary materials to be purchased and the work was completed by the firemen.

The original Belford fire station, where flooding often prevented the appliance from turning out.

Seahouses fire station was in a converted stable and harness room.

Seahouses fire station consisted of the stable and harness room of a hotel, previously requisitioned by the NFS. The premises were deemed to be quite inadequate and useless for a permanent station. The hotel proprietor was pressing for the building's return and it appeared that grave difficulty would be experienced when requisition ended unless alternative premises were found, which at the time did not seem likely.

The other fire stations were deemed to be reasonably suitable given minor alterations and therefore were not in urgent need of renewal. Blyth would be adequate given suitable imminent alterations. Gosforth, though small and without drill space, was sufficient but the control room and workshop were built on part of the Royalty cinema car park. The owners, anticipating that the area might be needed for more car park space, refused to renew the original lease negotiated with the NFS except on a quarterly tenancy. Wallsend was undergoing minor adaptations to the accommodation and although lacking in drill space was meeting the present requirements. Whitley Bay's prewar station required extensive repairs and adaptations and lacked drill space, and the council was asked to sell an additional area at the rear of the station where the drill tower stood. Allendale was acceptable subject to some alterations, such as raising the height of the appliance room to admit a standard type of fire appliance, and Haydon Bridge and Prudhoe, while not entirely satisfactory, were acceptable and no problems were envisaged in the future. In October, though, Prudhoe Urban District Council asked the county council whether the fire station could be released to provide a plumbers' and painters' store for the UDC in return for help in selecting alternative premises for the fire brigade. Unfortunately, owing to restrictions on capital expenditure and the more urgent cases in other parts of the county, the fire brigade declined to release the premises. The Berwick station was erected during the war on a requisitioned site and, although lacking in drill space, was otherwise satisfactory and the land was accordingly purchased. Amble station had been erected by the NFS on part of a site requisitioned by the Ministry of Works. The buildings here were semi-permanent but there was inadequate drill space. Rothbury was deemed suitable, being held on a lease that expired in 1961, although this too lacked suitable drill space. New doors had to be fitted to the appliance room, though, as the old ones fell off, injuring a child. At Wooler there was a garage held on an annual tenancy and a requisitioned cottage used as a watch room. The accommodation was considered to be not wholly suitable but acceptable in the circumstances, providing it could all be kept.

A suitable headquarters was also a major consideration in the brigade's post war building programme. The existing premises were occupied under an arrangement with the Ministry of Works that was due to expire at the end of 1952. Arrangements to purchase the building from the original owners had been unsuccessful and the chief fire officer now felt that it was important that the Fire Brigades Committee should consider that, even if construction of a new headquarters would be unlikely in the next few years, the selection of a suitable site should go ahead as soon as possible. It was envisaged that the new headquarters should incorporate an operational fire station and equipment store, a transport workshop and some housing. Considering the many factors in deciding the location of a new headquarters – including firemen's houses and civil defence obligations – it was concluded that there were only two areas which would satisfy the needs of the service. These were a site in the neighbourhood of Wideopen, north of Gosforth, or a location on the outskirts of Morpeth. One site investigated at Wideopen was rejected as there was nowhere close enough to Gosforth that would give adequate fire cover to the town and that was free from objection from the coal mining, highway and agricultural lobbies. Moreover, there was no urgency to replace Gosforth's fire station as it was owned by the county council and was not presenting any problems regarding tenure. Morpeth's fire station, however, was only a temporary building on a requisitioned site and would have needed replacing in the near future. It consisted of a hut, control room and garages. The accommodation was described as cramped

The original brigade control at The Grove, Gosforth, in 1952. On the wall at the right is the disposition board for updating the availability of the brigade's appliances and officers.

and inadequate for drill purposes, and on top of this, the owners were pressing for the land to be returned to them. For civil defence purposes it was suggested that it would be better to locate the headquarters at a further distance from Tyneside than was possible in the area north of Gosforth, so bearing all these factors in mind a site was sought on the outskirts of Morpeth, large enough to contain all of the facilities previously suggested. One was quickly identified, on the east side of the Great North Road, consisting of almost six acres, and negotiations were immediately started to secure the site. The civil defence consideration referred to Tyneside being a target area for air attacks in any future war.

Given the unsuitability of some of the fire stations, the council, being unable to find any other suitable premises, was forced to the conclusion that in nearly every case there was no practical alternative but to build entirely new stations on new sites. Many years would pass before the building programme reached fruition and in some cases it would never entirely do so.

From 4 April 1950 for three days the brigade was inspected by His Majesty's Inspector of Fire Services, Mr P.P. Booth, OBE, who examined in some detail the whole of the operational organisation. These Home Office Inspectorate visits occurred annually. Having viewed the brigade being tested under various conditions and undertaken many station inspections, the inspector expressed his 'satisfaction with the organisation and with the standard displayed by the brigade', although he did comment on the unsatisfactory situation in respect of station accommodation throughout the brigade. So concerned was the county council about the state of the fire stations that a memorandum was prepared and sent to the Home Office expressing a wish to send a deputation to London to discuss the situation. As luck would have it, the

Whitley Bay firemen parading in Oxford Street at the front of the fire station, because of the inadequate drill ground facilities. His Majesty's Inspector of the Fire Services, Percy Booth, and Chief Fire Officer Muir address the crews. The station's Austin escape carrying unit is still attired in its wartime grey livery, complete with wartime NFS codes.

acute position was relieved somewhat when the expiry of requisitioning powers was extended for a further twelve months to December 1953. A further extension to December 1960 gave the council even further breathing space. By the end of the year some progress had been made regarding station alterations and the seemingly unsuitable accommodation facilities, but the development plans for Blyth were thwarted when the Home Office declined to allow the brigade to build a first floor extension onto the station. Instead, a new fire station was built at Belford. The purchase of the site at Bellingham offered by the Duke of Northumberland was approved, but further approval was needed for construction to begin.

The total number of fire calls rose only slightly in 1950. There were eight large farm and haystack fires, most of which presented difficulties as far as adequate water supplies were concerned. Two horses were burned to death in a farm fire at Ashington and haystacks or barns were destroyed at Prospect Hill, Ponteland; Hartford East, Cramlington; West Farm, Earsdon; Six Mile Bridge, Seaton Burn; Corbridge; Shotton and Cresswell. Another serious fire involved an explosion on an RAF rescue boat moored at its base in Blyth harbour. The large quantity of fuel carried on the vessel contributed greatly to its destruction. The total sustained damage by fire in the county at the end of this year amounted to £35,410, of which £30,000 was attributed solely to the RAF fire.

Frequent training exercises took place throughout the county, especially in the forest regions of Kielder and Redesdale. The inherent risks in these areas prompted the chief fire officer and his staff to spend many hours devising plans and strategies that could be adopted should the large afforested areas become involved in fire.

Plane Trees Farm, Hexham, on 4 December 1949. Both Hexham crews are engaged in turning over hundreds of tons of hay in an effort to extinguish smouldering hot spots.

Heaps of straw and manure threaten to engulf Blyth Fire Brigade's prewar emergency tender and the station's utility van at Hartford East Farm near Cramlington.

The engine of this Royal Air Force aircraft rescue boat exploded and caught fire, resulting in the near destruction of the vessel at its Blyth base. Occurring in 1950 it was the brigade's most costly fire of the year.

A Forestry Commission Land Rover was used to assist with the siting of this trailer pump deep in the heart of Kielder Forest.

Thrunton Woods in March 1950. Forestry Commission Land Rovers prepare to convey two trailer pumps across the fells.

The use of radio was approved this year for the county's police force, and was scheduled to be in operation by the following year, and consideration was given for the inclusion of fire brigade vehicles within this scheme. The limited allocation of frequencies precluded the fire brigade from having a scheme of its own, so as a compromise an approach was made to the police authority with a view to concluding joint arrangements, subject to Home Office approval.

When 1951 dawned, many of the service's fire appliances and ancillary vehicles were still painted in the wartime grey livery and some of the prewar appliances were badly in need of a repaint. This included Gosforth's Bedford tender which was still adorned in its original prewar lime green colour scheme. Twenty-nine fire engines and trailer pumps were individually sent to an outside agency, Messrs M. Hubbick & Son of Newcastle, for repainting.

Recruitment to the AFS continued apace, and by May the force numbered 289 people. There was also an obligation for the brigade's full-time and retained men to undertake civil defence training. On top of this, measures had to be taken to ensure that an adequate supply of water was always available for combating fires caused by enemy action. More and more time was now being devoted to civil defence activities. In view of the increasing workload, it was decided that a specific officer should be delegated to co-ordinate the civil defence requirements. The establishment of the brigade was therefore increased by one additional officer position at station officer rank, and Sub Officer John Grigor from Wallsend was promoted to the post. An additional Austin towing vehicle was issued on free loan from the Home Office in view of the increasing numbers of AFS personnel. By August there were 322 individuals attached to the AFS in the county. The brigade was keen to recruit volunteers from the rural areas and visits were accordingly made to Amble, Seahouses and Rothbury accompanied by a Daylight cinema unit made available by the Central Office of Information. Twenty-four recruits were enrolled at

Gosforth men enjoy a welcome cup of tea while attending a farm fire at Six Mile Bridge in July 1950. The station's prewar Bedford tender is still displaying NFS insignia.

Wallsend's centenary celebrations. The town's old pump escape leads a parade of appliances through the town in an attempt to increase the establishment of the Auxiliary Fire Service.

A Home Office Fordson mobile recruiting exhibition attempts to swell the numbers of AFS recruits at Morpeth in 1951. By the looks of things it is being well patronised.

Amble and Seahouses but no success followed the efforts made at Rothbury. Further pressures were put onto the brigade when the Secretary of State announced that another recruitment programme directed towards national and local publicity was to commence in October and carry on through the autumn and winter.

The three new water tenders were all operational by November 1951. The Whitson model was assigned to Alnwick, the Carmichael one went to Berwick and the final one, from Miles, went to Morpeth. The firms that supplied the three machines all claimed features in bodywork which gave increased efficiency over rival products and, while it was agreed that all of them had commendable characteristics, extensive tests were carried out in order to select the most economic and efficient type suitable for the conditions encountered in Northumberland. The all-metal appliance constructed by Miles of Cheltenham was the one eventually selected to form the basis of the future fleet of fire engines for Northumberland. These Miles–bodied appliances marked something of a revolution in the design of fire engines. 'One huge locker enclosed by four light alloy roller shutters is a brief but not inaccurate description' of the new water tender delivered to Northumberland, as claimed in the magazine *Fire Protection and Accident Prevention Review*. The vehicle featured a light alloy body and was fitted with a 400-gallon water tank feeding a pair of hose reels. The design specification included materials to give the vehicle the lightest form of coachwork consistent with strength and the ability to withstand exceptionally hard usage, as well as a good road performance. Secondly the coachwork was designed to have a life span of fifteen years. This figure was greatly exceeded by the Northumberland machines. Other requirements were that the appliance should be able to negotiate very narrow thoroughfares in town and country as well as sharp corners, and should be capable of going over

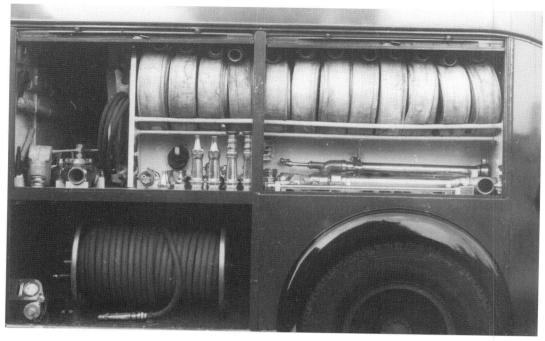

The abundance of locker space on the new Miles water tenders is amply illustrated in this picture. Only the water tenders had the forward 'transverse' locker, as illustrated.

The first of many Miles-bodied Commer water tenders in service with Northumberland. A Morris Sigmund trailer pump was towed behind and a dismountable one was housed on the rear of the appliance. Later the entire water tender fleet would undergo a modernisation programme.

The original rear bodywork of the Miles water tenders housed a Sigmund trailer pump unit, connected to the 400-gallon water tank by a short length of reinforced hose.

rough country at relatively high speeds. The cab featured excellent visibility with wraparound side windows, headroom of 5ft 4in and seating for a crew of six with access via jack-knife type doors on each side. According to the manufacturers, these appliances had 'the best driving visibility ever', the deep curved screens and very small pillars completely eliminating blind spots, unlike one of the previously delivered appliances that had raised some concern with blind spots in the driving position. The total weight of the vehicle less crew was 6 tons 12cwt and it could accelerate from 0 to 40mph in 31 seconds. Power came from a Rootes six-cylinder underfloor-mounted petrol engine. Although different specifications were available for the machine, Northumberland's specifications called for pumping equipment consisting of a demountable Morris-Sigmund pump to be mounted at the rear with facilities for towing a similar trailer-mounted unit. A further three water tenders and one multi-purpose pump with 50ft wheeled escape were ordered for delivery in 1952, together with three more Austin A40 utility vans for use by operational station officers.

Fires still occurred, and in March a fire at Anne's Café, Alnwick, saw the local brigade being greeted with the spectacular sight of flames shooting from the first-floor windows of the flat above. In the greatest tradition of the firefighter, the blaze was quickly quenched. In October the Collieries Fire Brigade had to seek reinforcements from the county when fire raged through the roofs of four terraced houses at Fifth Row, Ashington. Training exercises continued unabated, with a large one taking place at Kielder Forest in March. This location was also the venue of an Institute of Fire Engineering meeting when fire officers from various parts of the country were given a tour of the area and enlightened on the arrangements that were in place to protect the heavily forested areas should fire break out. The Forestry Commission had its own fire appliances

Anne's Café, Alnwick, in March 1951. The first floor is obviously well alight. The town's original open topped Bedford motor pump is in the foreground.

at this time, consisting of light trailer pumps towed by the Commission's Land Rovers. Later in the year the organisation, in conjunction with the fire brigade, began experiments with a unique vehicle suitably adapted to be able to traverse the more remote areas of Northumberland's forests.

As a contrast from the forestry regions, 'Exercise Industry' took place in March at Blyth harbour, when many appliances and personnel were mobilised to the port. This exercise stemmed from a notice issued by the Home Office drawing the attention of fire authorities to their responsibility for ensuring adequate supplies of water for the purpose of fighting fires in ships in port. At this time there were significant risks at the port of Blyth. The port had had the distinction of being the biggest coal-exporting port in the world and there were major imports of timber pit props for the coal mining industry. Additionally, there was a large shipbuilding and repair yard on the south side and a busy ship-breaking yard at Cambois.

The brigade had attempted to standardise vehicles by acquiring Austin cars. These were formerly obtained through agreed priority delivery with the Secretary of State, but this agreement was terminated in early 1952, resulting in an estimated waiting list of between three and four years for the delivery of further Austin cars. One more car was required to complete the establishment, however, and as the Rootes Group promised early delivery of a Hillman Minx car at an almost equivalent price, one of these models was duly ordered.

It can be seen that the first three years of the County Fire Brigade had been a continual struggle to make improvements in almost every aspect of operation, from appliances to buildings. None of the improvements could have happened without the complete co-operation of the entire workforce, from the administrative staff through to the operational crews. The nation's

This former military bren gun carrier underwent a number of conversions to test its suitability in the terrain of Kielder Forest. Northumberland's senior fire officers and an army officer put the vehicle through its paces in March 1951.

firemen, however, were not a content lot. Long working hours and poor conditions in stations, not only in Northumberland but elsewhere in the country, started to take their toll. In support of a claim for increased pay, the Fire Brigades Union (FBU) called upon their members to abstain collectively from performing any duties other than emergencies from Monday 19 November 1952 for three days. The Secretary of State informed fire authorities by telegram that 'he looked upon them to carry out their responsibilities to maintain an efficient fire service' and expressed his opinion that actions by members of brigades along the lines suggested by the FBU would be a serious breach of the Fire Services (Discipline) Regulations 1948. Despite this the dispute went ahead and appropriate charges had to be laid against fifty-eight firemen for refusing to obey lawful orders given to them by their superior officers. The stations affected were Blyth, Gosforth, Newburn, Wallsend and Whitley Bay. After suitable deliberations by a sub-committee of the Fire Authority, the charges were proven and stoppages of pay ranging from £1 to £3 were imposed on the men. The dispute was perhaps not all in vain, however, as in February new scales of pay were awarded to the nation's firemen.

Since recruitment for the AFS began, twenty-six members had enrolled at Ashington. It had not been practical for them to undergo training at the National Coal Board's rescue station, so a county school was used instead, which was also not altogether satisfactory. Premises known as 'The Buildings', High Market, Ashington, were admirably suitable for accommodating two towing vehicles and pumps together with facilities for a watch room and store, and were available on an annual tenancy. With a 75 per cent grant available from the Home Office, it was strongly recommended that the premises be acquired. A station had already been established at Bedlington in a garage made available at no cost to the brigade by Bedlingtonshire District

Council. By the end of the year the number of people enrolled in the AFS had reached a staggering 986, but resignations brought the number down to 803, comprising 695 men and 108 women. Door-to-door canvassing had produced 511 recruits of this total, which exceeded the initial recruitment target by 130. Northumberland gained the distinction of having enrolled more recruits than any other brigade in Great Britain. Undoubtedly, this large expansion raised many problems concerning the organisation, equipment and training of the service. Storage accommodation for uniforms was made available by the Civil Defence Committee at Darras Hall and schools were hired for training purposes. An additional seven auxiliary towing vehicles, two major trailer pumps and two light trailer pumps were loaned from the Home Office to cope with the expansion.

An unusually high number of injuries resulting from fires and other incidents was reported at the February Fire Brigades Committee meeting. In three cases injuries received from fires proved fatal and in three other cases severe burns and shock necessitated the removal of the injured to hospital.

The installation of wireless telephony in some of the appliances was completed by April and proved in practice to be an aid to efficiency. The radio scheme was shared with Northumberland Constabulary. All radio messages were transmitted through the police control at Morpeth by way of a radio link between that site and the fire brigade headquarters, with the result that the fire control received all police messages as well as fire brigade messages. The receipt of so much irrelevant information at the brigade control was distracting and said to increase the possibility of actual fire brigade messages being overlooked, so to alleviate the problem a land line between

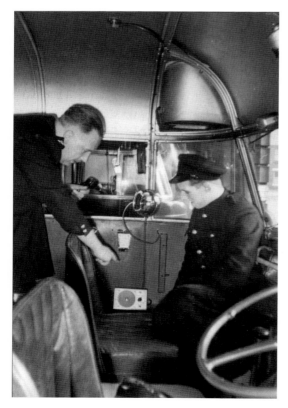

Early radio microphones were fist-type units. They were later replaced by telephone-type handsets.

the police and fire brigade headquarters was provided which eliminated the constant cacophony of police 'all station' messages. Unfortunately, this system did not work on the fire brigade mobiles, which had to endure the police messages until the brigade eventually acquired its own radio scheme as additional frequencies became available. The unavoidable interception of police messages led to a memorandum being issued to all personnel reminding them of the need to maintain confidentiality regarding these police radio transmissions. The brigade control was allocated the call sign 'M2LB-F' and the mobiles were allocated numbers preceded by 'LB'. Numbers 1–49 were police call signs and following on from these were the fire brigade vehicles.

Her Majesty's Inspector of Fire Services, Percy Booth, OBE, was back again in May 1952 expressing his satisfaction with both the organisation and standard displayed. This year an exercise was laid on at Kielder in conjunction with the Forestry Commission.

In August the second batch of three new water tenders were received at the workshops and were later allocated to Hexham, Newburn and Gosforth. Also delivered with this batch was the brigade's first new multi-purpose pump, a development of the Miles water tender, of which Northumberland received the prototype. This new appliance was based on similar lines to the company's existing water tenders but was equipped to carry a 50ft wheeled escape as well as a 35ft extension ladder, hook ladder and short extension ladder. The pump was a fixed unit of Dennis manufacture, mounted at the rear and capable of delivering water at a rate of 500 gallons per minute. When the appliance replacement programme was complete every full-time fire station would have a pair of Miles Commers, a multi-purpose pump and water tender. Wallsend received the prototype model, replacing their former UDC Dennis Big 4 Braidwood pump escape. The delivery of Wallsend's new appliance meant that some unpredicted additional

The prototype Commer-Miles multi-purpose pump was delivered to the Brigade in 1952 and allocated to Wallsend. A fireman demonstrates the balancing arrangements of the 50ft Bayley wheeled escape. The release mechanism, behind the rear wheel, was later moved to the hose reel compartment.

expenditure was incurred, as the appliance room entry had to be widened and new doors made to enable the machine to be housed inside the station. The delivery of the new appliances resulted in four former NFS self-propelled pumps becoming surplus to requirements. Because of the special design of these vehicles they commanded relatively little value on the open market and were therefore exchanged by the Home Office for eight light trailer pumps. This was a particularly advantageous deal for the brigade as it avoided having to buy pumps for fitting to the water tenders. The first of the former UDC fire engines were disposed of at this time. Wallsend's Dennis pump escape went to Trembles Demolition Company's yard at Benton, and Gosforth's old Leyland limousine motor pump went to Snippersgate service station, Easington Lane, County Durham, where it was converted to a breakdown recovery vehicle. This appliance was originally of Braidwood-style design but was rebuilt as a limousine during the war following an accident.

Plans to start constructing new fire stations at Belford and Bellingham were put on hold because the Secretary of State suspended indefinitely all fire service building projects other than housing, which involved the use of steel. It was not all bad news, however. The plans to go ahead with Alnwick's new fire station on 3.8 acres of land owned by the Duke of Northumberland had been passed and, as it was originally proposed to work the station under day manning arrangements, the building specifications included the construction of eleven houses. The county architect was now asked to prepare plans and estimates as quickly as possible for the preparation of the site to begin. The acquisition of land on a 6-acre site adjoining the Great North Road near the county police headquarters at Morpeth was approved in principle at this time by both the council and the Home Office, but the owner of the land, on being approached, stated that

The delivery of the Miles appliances led to the early withdrawal of some of the former NFS appliances. This rudimentary Fordson water tender was one of them and bears no resemblance to its modern counterparts.

he was not prepared to sell this area unless the council also purchased an additional 7 acres. This additional land was an adjoining field which would have been severed from the Great North Road by the proposed site. Despite an assurance that the council would provide an accommodation road, the owner would not waver. The council's hand was forced. All of the land was bought, giving the council its site for the new headquarters complex.

Serious fires continued this year, with the Army Drill Hall at Seaton Deleval suffering severe damage in August when a fire in the upper floors of the building, which also housed some of the county's ambulances, spread to the roof. Four pumps from Blyth, Whitley Bay and Gosforth attended the call and, by midnight, thirty minutes from the origination of the call, the fire was under control. Earlier on in the year, in April, Alnwick crews attended a spectacular road accident, which unfortunately resulted in the death of a petrol tanker driver when the vehicle he was driving collided with a tree at Falloden Mill near Chathill and burst into flames.

The night of 31 January 1953 saw the region struck by exceptionally severe weather, which resulted in fifteen calls for assistance owing to roofs being stripped, chimney pots crashing through roofs and sea flooding etc. Being classed as special service calls and theoretically liable to charging, the Fire Brigades Committee very benevolently consented to waive any charges on the grounds that the services rendered were essentially humanitarian. Earlier in the month the Hexham area suffered severe flooding, and for their efforts in rescuing a man trapped by flood waters at Corbridge, Sub Officers Harris and Parker and Fireman Adamson were awarded commendations 'for displaying courage, determination and a disregard for their own personal safety during the rescue'. The rest of Northumberland got off relatively lightly. Worse weather conditions were reported in other parts of the country, especially along the coast of East

This road tanker was totally destroyed by fire at Falloden Mill near Alnwick in April 1953.

During the winter of 1953 Divisional Officer Harkins and a contingent of firemen were sent to East Anglia to assist with flood relief work. Here, the contingent is seen on its return on 11 February 1953.

Anglia and Essex, where floods claimed hundreds of lives and were the worst in living memory. Unsurprisingly, the fire brigades in these areas were stretched to their limits. Appeals for help were made to all parts of the country and, always willing to oblige, Northumberland County Council offered help, which was gratefully accepted. A contingent of three pumps, one service van, one towing vehicle, a staff car and twelve personnel under the command of Divisional Officer J.B. Harkins was promptly assembled and dispatched to Lincolnshire on Wednesday 11 February as part of a detachment represented by all brigades in the region. The principal objective of the detachment was to provide an insurance against the consequences of more flooding. Fortunately this did not occur and the work was confined to a pumping operation, which involved the removal of several million gallons of water to aid further drainage. To date this feat has never been exceeded and it is doubtful whether Northumberland County appliances will ever travel this distance again.

A situation that Muir had feared since taking up his post in Northumberland occurred in the early hours of 25 March 1953. It was the first real test of the brigade's mobilising capabilities at large and prolonged incidents. On this day the brigade was called to the privately owned area of forest to the north of Belford at Shiellaw Crags. An area approaching 100 acres of heather caught fire during 'controlled burning' by one of the estate's tenants but it was not until the fire

The remoteness of Shiellaw Crags is typical of some of the rural parts of Northumberland. The location featured two ten-pump fires within days of each other.

threatened some standing timber that the fire brigade was alerted. A high wind and low humidity aided the rapid spread of the fire and it soon became obvious that a serious fire was developing. Ten pumping appliances were immediately mobilised to the scene, despite extremely poor water supplies, and the council's policy over the previous four years of acquiring water tenders with 400 gallons of water paid off, although some of the machines had to travel considerable distances to reach the fire, especially from Gosforth. The fire was brought under control in a little over six hours, but was not finally extinguished until three days later. Of 1,000 acres of standing timber that was threatened, some 40 acres of one to four-year-old trees and 4 acres of ten to twenty-year-old trees were severely damaged. A total of 135 officers and men were employed in the operation. Three days later, just as this fire had been finally extinguished, another but entirely separate area of the same estate was reported as being on fire, again following 'controlled burning'. The brigade was called shortly after midday on the 28th, and although this fire was halted five hours later, operations continued until 6.45 p.m. on 1 April. The same problems occurred here as at Shiellaw Crags and again a total of ten water tenders were mobilised to deal with the situation. In view of the serious nature of these fires the Fire Brigades Committee arranged a joint meeting with representatives of the Fire Authority and the County Agricultural Executive Committee, the National Farmers' Union and the Country Landowners' Association to discuss what measures could be taken to minimise the risk and prevent the spread of fire in moorland areas. The Inspector of Fire Services was visiting the brigade at the time of these fires so was given a first-hand view of the brigade in action. As circumstances permitted visits were also made to some of the fire stations in the county, notably Wallsend, Newburn and Berwick. This was the last year of His Majesty's Inspectorate, for on 2 June 1953 a new monarch was crowned, Queen Elizabeth II. The occasion was one of great jubilation for the country, with

His Majesty's Inspector, Percy Booth, inspects Wallsend's watch outside the swimming baths, next to the fire station.

Wallsend personnel very graciously decorated the fire station during the 1953 Coronation ceremony. The station has just taken delivery of its second Commer appliance.

many celebratory events taking place. The personnel at Wallsend fire station joined in with spirit and decorated the station to commemorate the event.

The same year, orders were placed for four more multi-purpose pumps, or pump escapes as they were later termed, all on Commer chassis with coachwork by Miles. Also this year, with the approval of the Home Office and under the aegis of the Chief Fire Officers' Association, a national technical quiz competition was instituted with the objective of encouraging and furthering technical study. The competition was open to both full-time and part-time retained members and it was pleasing to note that every station with retained personnel entered the competition. Alnwick's team earned the distinction of being the brigade's finalists, qualifying them to compete with the finalists from other brigades. Those teams that reached the finals ultimately went forward to the national finals held at the Fire Service College, Dorking. For two years running the retained team at Alnwick won the regional class in the National Technical Quiz and thus qualified to enter the district finals at Sheffield. Another source of entertainment introduced during the year was annual drill competitions, whereby crews from all of the brigade's stations, including AFS personnel, entered teams in various hose-running and ladder-pitching competitions. The best teams were awarded trophies and the competitions usually ended with some light entertainment for the audience, such as water football games.

Haydon Bridge retained unit was mobilised just after midnight on 21 April following a request for assistance at Haydon Bridge railway station where an accident involving twelve tanks of ammoniacal liquor had occurred. Five tanks had ruptured and as a heavy concentration of gas was causing danger over a wide area, it was necessary to evacuate a number of people from their homes. Firemen wearing breathing apparatus attempted to plug the fractured tanks but

Berwick firemen undergo escape drill in March 1953. The three firemen have been completely lifted off the ground as they raise the escape ladder from its securing mountings.

Haydon Bridge firemen proudly pose for the camera in front of the town's fire station, a requisitioned brick outbuilding.

this proved impossible. However, continuous sprays of diffused water diluted the concentration of gas in the atmosphere.

There was still time for exercises, and as usual the forest regions provided suitable training areas. Redesdale featured in March and Wark Forest in both October and December. It was during these exercises that Chief Officer Muir was able to evaluate some of his inventions and this year experiments took place with 6-inch fibreglass and plywood pipes as devices for conveying large quantities of water to remote sites. In the near future other developments would put a halt to these experiments, but would not dampen the chief's enthusiasm for further development of new firefighting techniques.

Northumberland's firemen were now equipped with the new fibreglass helmets and the uniform issue was supplemented this year by the addition of socks and pullovers. The pullovers, navy blue with 'NCFB' in red, were to be replaced at four-yearly intervals for the full-time men and every nine years for the retained members.

The beginning of 1954 saw the brigade on the receiving end of some unfortunate adverse publicity following a serious fire at the Station Hotel, Whitley Bay, on 7 January. After the fire, the brigade received a letter from Whitley Bay Urban District Council referring to rumours which had been persisting in the town in connection with this fire. On top of this, adverse statements

Above: *Muir's fibreglass and plywood piping undergoing pressure tests at one of the Northumberland forests.*

Right: *This Northumberland fireman is displaying the all-black uniform that became the norm from 1952 onwards. In the future years, yellow would add some contrast.*

Next page: *The aftermath of the fire at the Station Hotel, Whitley Bay. Reinforcements from Tynemouth were called in to assist Whitley Bay. The brigade was exonerated from all blame following criticisms raised about its efficiency at this incident.*

appeared in the local press. The county council was requested to investigate suggestions that the brigade's equipment was unsuitable and that the hydrants were not in order, and also for a report on the training arrangements for the fire brigade personnel. The investigation was undertaken in accordance with the UDC's wishes and after a full investigation of all the circumstances of the fire, the committee unanimously decided that the rumours referred to, which – despite opportunities being given – no one was prepared to substantiate, were completely without foundation. Both the equipment provided at Whitley Bay Fire Station and the fire hydrants were in excellent working order. The council was also satisfied that all members of the brigade were adequately trained. The press statements were proven to be devoid of any foundation and a public statement to that effect was issued to the people of Whitley Bay. The Fire Brigades Committee decided to place on record that the officers and men of Whitley Bay Fire Brigade performed their duty efficiently and well in circumstances requiring tenacity, courage and a high standard of training, skill and personal endeavour. The committee gave instructions for a letter to be sent to the station officer and men expressing complete confidence in them, and offering its appreciation, which committee members were 'sure is shared by the general public, of the efficient and courageous way in which the fire was so effectively dealt with'.

Two more former UDC appliances were sold this year. Alnwick's former Bedford 16hp motor pump and Hexham's attractive Dennis Ace both went together with three Dennis 350/500 gallon trailer pumps, the latter raising £70 more per item than the Hexham pump. Some shrewd dealings also took place with the disposal of two Fordson pump escapes. These appliances had a limited value on the open market so they were offered to the Home Office in exchange for ten wheelbarrow pumps. The estimated price to be attained for the pump escapes was £30 each while the value of the ten wheelbarrow pumps was £500! Also leaving the brigade at this time was Divisional Officer Roland Noble, formerly in charge of the North and South Divisions. He left to take up an appointment as deputy chief fire officer of Leicester Fire Brigade. He was to return to the region some years later to take up the prestigious position of chief fire officer of Newcastle & Gateshead Joint Fire Service.

Plans for the new headquarters had now been approved, but were amended at this time to include twenty-nine houses to accommodate twenty fire station and workshop personnel and nine headquarters officers, including the chief fire officer. The construction of the new two-bay station at Bellingham, originally approved in principle by the council in 1949, was now finally sanctioned by the Home Office. The need for a replacement station at Rothbury was still a pressing matter, however. This station consisted of a garage with a loft above, but was too small to accommodate one of the new appliances that were being introduced. On top of this, the only means of access was via a common right of way consisting of a narrow entry between houses. As the lease for the premises was due to expire in 1961, the need for alternative premises was urgent, but the search for another site on reasonably level ground was proving fruitless. There was some light at the end of the tunnel when the rural district council offered the brigade

Both of these subjects left the brigade in 1954. Divisional Officer Roland Noble went to Leicestershire Fire Brigade, and the former Alnwick Bedford motor pump went for disposal.

The former Hexham RDC Dennis Ace motor pump was sold in 1954 for £30. Had it survived it would undoubtedly had become a collector's item. It is pictured in 1952 arriving at an exercise held for His Majesty's Inspector of Fire Services.

Rothbury's second fire station was in a former bus company garage.

the opportunity to join with it in acquiring some premises consisting of a large stone-built house with a cottage attached, a large former bus garage, a series of lock-up garages and sundry outhouses. The council was considering the acquisition of the house as council offices and using part of the garage for housing council vehicles. For the fire brigade it was suggested that the garage would have provided an immediate and more suitable alternative to the present station and the site could also be used for the erection of a new fire station in due course.

An unusual special service call occurred on 9 February 1954 when Newburn Fire Station received an urgent call from a doctor attending a patient at Throckley. At the scene the brigade was required to set up a resuscitator and administer oxygen to a patient who was then sufficiently revived to enable him to be taken to hospital. An appreciation of the speed and efficiency with which this service was rendered was later received from the doctor concerned. All of the brigade's first turn-out appliances carried Novox resuscitators, while at this time the ambulance service did not carry any such equipment.

In July a fire broke out in a prefabricated house on a housing estate at Seghill destroying the building completely within 17 minutes. The houses on either side also caught fire and were badly burned. It was found that the walls of this type of prefabricated house were made from processed sawdust board, which was highly inflammable. So alarmed was the brigade by the rapid destruction of the building that details of the fire and construction were sent to relevant government departments and Seaton Valley Urban District Council, suggesting the actions to be taken to reduce the likelihood of fire in these types of houses.

The flue is the only thing remaining of a prefabricated house that caught fire at Seghill in July 1954. A group of interested spectators looks on as firemen sift through the debris.

The brigade continued to keep itself in a high state of efficiency and readiness, and exercises continued in the forest regions with another Institute of Fire Engineering meeting being held at Kyloe in July, an exercise at Wark in the following month and a large combined AFS exercise at Swan Hunter and Wigham Richardson shipbuilders at Wallsend during the same month. New appliances continued to arrive and for this financial year an additional three pump escapes were ordered. For the first time a water tender was bought on a Dennis chassis with Miles bodywork. The Dennis appliance was based on the company's popular 'F8' series, with a six cylinder Rolls Royce B80 petrol engine but unusually fitted at the brigade's request with Miles bodywork to conform to the similar pattern of the larger Commer appliances. A total of ten Dennis engines were eventually ordered, all for service at the retained stations. Apart from the front assembly they were basically a smaller version of the Commer water tenders, and were fitted out with the same locker and pump arrangements. The new pump escapes that were now arriving were much larger appliances than had been used in the county fire stations, and subsequent deliveries resulted in many fire stations having to undergo alterations to headrooms so that the appliances could fit inside. The problem with the doors at Wallsend had been readily resolved, but the delivery of Gosforth's new pump escape in 1954 presented more problems than others. The entrance to the station was through an archway in the Council Chambers buildings, preventing the new arrival from entering the appliance room. It was totally impractical to raise the archway, so the roadway into the fire station was lowered by twelve inches. Height restrictions in the appliance room also posed problems and to resolve this, channels were made into the flooring and a notch was cut into the door lintel to allow sufficient clearance for the head of the escape ladder. The floor at Newburn also had to be lowered, as did the appliance bay at Hexham, for similar reasons. After many years of negotiations and setbacks, extensions and adaptations to Whitley Bay's fire station

Chief Fire Officer Muir in the heart of Northumberland's forest with an entourage of guests at one of the regional Institute of Fire Engineering meetings.

Above: *The first of the Rolls-Dennis water tenders was delivered in 1954 for Haltwhistle fire station. The smart machine is pictured in the Royalty cinema car park just after delivery. A further nine were delivered over the following years.*

Right: *Hexham fire station during escape drills. The entrance to the multi-purpose pump bay had been raised to allow clearance for the wheeled escape of the multi-purpose pump.*

were finally approved. These alterations consisted of the erection of a drill tower, extension of the drill yard and the construction of an access way into the station from the rear yard. The plans also entailed the erection of a new building on a site next to the fire station.

In the meantime, fires still had to be attended to. The Haltwhistle retained unit was kept busy when the historic Blenkinsop Castle near Greenhead, almost on the Cumberland border, was gutted by fire, and there was more to come. In the early morning of 14 December, the brigade control received a request from Durham County Fire Brigade for the provision of two pumps to attend a major fire in Sunderland. The large Jopling's department store in the city centre, packed with Christmas goods, was alight from end to end and the Sunderland Fire Brigade, which was valiantly battling to prevent the fire encroaching on neighbouring buildings, now required a total of fifteen pumps to supplement the town's four pumps. Water tenders from Gosforth and Wallsend were promptly dispatched on what was a typical damp, foggy December night. Gosforth's appliance was the most distant of all stations involved at this conflagration. With no knowledge of the area at all, fortune smiled on the driver when at Felling on Tyne the tail lights of Dunston's towing vehicle were sighted and thus the Gosforth machine was fortuitously guided to the fire. Fourteen minutes after these two appliances had been mobilised a further assistance message, calling for an additional five pumps, was transmitted, resulting in Newburn's water tender being promptly assigned to the long list of reinforcements joining others from South Shields, Newcastle & Gateshead, Durham County and the Coal Board. The fire was not brought under control until 5 a.m. and the Northumberland appliances were finally released and on their way home by 7.30 a.m. This was the first occasion that Northumberland appliances had travelled the distance to Sunderland but it was not to be the last.

The interior of Blenkinsop Castle, Haltwhistle, was totally gutted by fire in May 1954.

This is the inferno that greeted Northumberland's crews after they had travelled the long distance to Sunderland in December 1954. (Courtesy of Sunderland Fire Brigade)

Whitley Bay's wartime Austin pump escape, pictured at the workshop, was withdrawn in 1954 when a new Commer was delivered. The Barton front-mounted pump was a conversion, fitted in 1953.

The remainder of 1954 was relatively uneventful except that two more prewar UDC fire engines were sold as new replacements were delivered. These were both Bedford towing vehicles, one originally supplied to Gosforth and the other from Blyth. At the end of the year the brigade had attended a total of 1,305 calls. Actual fires totaled 663. There were 231 chimney fires and 123 false alarms incorporated in the total. The busiest station was again Gosforth, with 268 calls, followed by Wallsend and Whitley Bay. The busiest retained station was Rothbury with 17; the quietest, Allendale with 4.

By 1955 the numbers of AFS personnel had increased to 818, made up of 718 men and 100 women. The numbers fluctuated somewhat owing to frequent resignations, many of them joining the ranks of the full-time or retained sections of the brigade. It was not always easy to stimulate and maintain enthusiasm in such a large group of volunteers, so in August it was decided to establish a local camp suitable for the collective training of these people. The tenancy of four Forestry Commission huts at Kielder was secured and after some modification and reconditioning, this venue became a regular weekend retreat for the AFS. It was hoped ultimately to establish a permanent AFS station at the site, manned by a locally recruited workforce of volunteers. The camp had provision for accommodating up to fifty trainees and, by the end of November, four weekend courses had already been held, attended by fifty-one auxiliary firemen in addition to full-time men. Recruitment of AFS staff still went on and frequent exercises continued to be held in the more populated areas of the county in order to publicise the work and importance of the organisation. The increasing commitment of the government to civil defence saw the start of a major vehicle-building programme, which enabled a large number of new vehicles to be allotted to the country's fire brigades. It was under this programme that the county received its first 'Green Goddess' fire engine. These self propelled pumps or emergency pumps based on Bedford chassis were supplied to the brigade in both two-wheel and four-wheel drive versions and were finished

Kielder AFS camp in 1955, with the wooden huts used for billeting the men. One of the new Home Office Land Rovers can be seen parked in front.

The country's former wartime AFS fleet was considerably updated in 1954. Here an impressive array of Green Goddess emergency pumps are pictured while attending a training exercise at Swan Hunter and Wigham Richardson shipyards, Wallsend, in August 1954.

in dark green livery with red titling. The theory behind the Civil Defence's obligations in times of war was to move vehicle and manpower resources to the scenes of devastation that may have followed a nuclear attack. The fleets or mobile columns also included many other appliance types, such as hose layers, transportable water units, communications and field telephone units and personnel carriers. There were even motorcycles to be used by convoy dispatch riders. The country's AFS was now provided with the most modern and up-to-date pieces of equipment. The delivery of these units saw most of the trailer pumps and Austin towing vehicles returned to the Home Office stores at Tranwell near Morpeth, although some of the latter were retained until the organisation was disbanded some years later.

Problems at the fire brigade's headquarters at The Grove caused some additional unplanned expenditure in the early part of 1955, when it was discovered that the dreaded timber beetle was causing serious damage by eating through the timber joists of the adjoining cottage. The least affected parts were treated with insecticide but it was necessary to renew part of the flooring and some of the supporting joists. Approval was given this year for the purchase of five more fire appliances, three Dennis water tenders and two all-alloy hose carrier/salvage tender bodies for mounting onto Bedford 2–3-ton chassis. The order for the two Bedfords was later replaced by an order for two Commer-Karrier Gamecock chassis. These two appliances were a new design for the brigade and were essentially a Karrier chassis with four door Rootes cab as supplied to many municipal authorities for use as dustcarts. For the fire brigade the chassis and cabs were sent off to Miles at Cheltenham, where a box-type body with roller-shutter locker enclosures were fitted. The purpose of the appliances was to ferry personnel and large amounts

Six of these Karrier Gamecock hose layer/salvage tenders were delivered to Northumberland. This Hexham vehicle was the last of the six. They were all later converted to emergency tenders.

of hose to forest and moorland fires. They were fitted with a hose reel pump and single hose reel, small water tank and had provision for towing a trailer pump. A total of six were ordered over the following three years and they were assigned to Alnwick, Bellingham, Berwick, Hexham, Morpeth and Rothbury.

An interesting interlude for Gosforth's firemen came in April and May when they were required during these two months to attend Newcastle's Woolsington Airport on the occasions when airliners were landing and taking off. The airport's sole fire tender had become unserviceable and the attendance of Gosforth's fire engine enabled the airport to remain operational. The service was very generously provided free of charge. The airport later purchased a Bedford Miles water/foam tender, similar to the county's appliances but with four-wheel drive. Also in April, the former Superintendent of the old Gosforth Urban District Council Fire Brigade passed away. Mr Jack Hann took over the running of the brigade from the renowned Superintendent Fred Coney, and together they were responsible for the high state of efficiency and order of the brigade that became part of the County Fire Authority in 1948. Mr Hann retired on medical grounds in 1944 after completing twenty-five years' service. His career was cut short in January 1941 when he fell from the canopy of the Royalty cinema during air-raid watching duties and was confined to hospital for several weeks. Thereafter his health deteriorated rapidly until eventually he was compelled to retire. The following year Fireman Charles Byrne of Gosforth passed away following a long illness. Mr Byrne had been in the fire brigade since 1938 and was unusually given a full service funeral, fortunately a rare event in Northumberland. The former Newburn UDC's Leyland motor pump was used as the hearse for this sombre occasion.

Right: *Former Gosforth Superintendent Jack Hann passed away in April 1955.*

Below: *Former Gosforth fireman Cyril Byrne is carried to his last resting place on the old Newburn Leyland motor pump in 1956.*

At the beginning of 1956 the three new Rolls Royce-powered Dennis water tenders had been delivered and were assigned to Rothbury, Prudhoe and Amble, making surplus three former NFS towing vehicles which were immediately put on the disposal list. Three more similar appliances were ordered later in the year, together with a further two hose carrier/salvage tenders. The brigade radio scheme was extended this year when a further ten mobile wireless stations were acquired on loan from the Home Office meaning that every full-time station had two wireless-equipped appliances. The retained stations would be next on the list for equipping with radio facilities.

Eleven of the county's recruited firemen were sent to the Regional Training School at Felling and once again firemen from Northumberland excelled. Former retained fireman Fred Trainer from Gosforth was awarded the silver axe for being the best recruit on the course and Fireman Alf Crossman, also from Gosforth, was awarded second place.

Major problems occurred in July in the Ashington area when the National Coal Board, which provided cover for Ashington and its surrounds, informed the council that because of a dispute between the board and members of its fire and rescue brigades, the brigade had declined to fight surface fires after 8 a.m. on 11 July. In view of this, the board considered that unless the dispute was speedily resolved they would be obliged to give the appropriate three months' notice and terminate all previous agreements. In this event the board offered to assist the council in any way that they could to provide a temporary fire station at Ashington. Emergency plans had to be promptly made to equip and man a temporary station in the event of the dispute going ahead, and interim arrangements were made to provide fire cover for Ashington from Morpeth, Blyth and Amble stations. The matter was not resolved in the

The delivery of the new Dennis and Karrier appliances saw the gradual replacement of these wartime Austin auxiliary towing vehicles.

Ashington Coal Board's impressive Leyland Terrier major pump backs into quarters on the main street in Ashington. Agreements with the Coal Board to provide fire cover were terminated in 1956.

way that the county council had hoped and the situation became more critical on 1 January 1956 when the National Coal Board gave notice to terminate the agreement completely. The situation was now considered in greater depth and it was decided that as an interim measure, duly approved by the Home Office, the brigade establishment would be increased by ten men, which, together with additional resources, would enable one appliance to be dispatched to respond to calls in the more densely populated parts of the area. Although this proposal provided a reasonable standard of cover for the area, it was not the complete answer, and approval was sought for the erection of a new fire station. A suggestion by Newbiggin-by-the-Sea Urban District Council that the proposed new fire station would be more conveniently sited at North Seaton was rejected in favour of the original suggestion to site the new fire station at Ashington. In the meantime, Chief Fire Officer Muir continued to negotiate with the Coal Board for a temporary agreement under which the board's fire and rescue brigade would provide a turnout in the Ashington area pending the arrival of the county brigade from Morpeth. Agreement was in fact reached quite amicably between the Coal Board and the union representing the rescue brigadesmen, both recommending that fire cover should be restored. However, the brigadesmen themselves intimated that they were not prepared to undertake the additional duties involved. It was thus decided that further attempts at negotiation would have served no useful purpose and the council was left with no other alternative but to provide its own arrangements for fire cover. To alleviate the problems in the short-term, the AFS station at Ashington was adapted to serve as the town's regular fire station. In order to make the place habitable for the firemen the station was equipped with a new hot water system, dormitory accommodation and cooking facilities.

Morpeth crews spring into action at the annual pump competitions. The 1955 event was held in the grounds of Alnwick Castle.

More floods hit the region in August and early September 1956 resulting in the brigade receiving twenty-three calls for assistance. Again all charges were waived. The government was still committed to publicising the Civil Defence organisation and to recruiting more members, and towards the end of the year all fire authorities were asked to exploit a national publicity campaign being arranged for early October. To this end plans were drawn up for a mobile AFS unit to conduct a series of exercises in towns where there were full-time fire stations. Details were advertised in local newspapers where it was hoped that the publicity would stimulate recruitment. Further recruiting campaigns occurred later in the year and one such campaign, directed mainly at industrial groups in Wallsend, Blyth and Ashington, resulted in thirty volunteers being recruited. These campaigns consisted of demonstrations of various items of AFS equipment and appliances that were displayed outside the shipyards at Wallsend and Blyth.

Although the replacement for Gosforth Fire Station had not been deemed to be as urgent as other stations, a site was offered on a new development in the Regent Farm area of Gosforth that provided enough space for a fire station and two houses. Too good an opportunity to miss, the site was acquired, meaning that in the future the building of a new station could go ahead immediately it was required. When the county council inherited Gosforth's fire station in 1948, with it came the UDC's mortuary which was located in a room adjacent to the appliance room. Part of the duties of the firemen was to assist with mortuary duties, for which some additional remuneration was awarded. In August 1957 the mortuary was thankfully relocated to a new self-contained building at Three Mile Bridge. The vacant mortuary room at the fire station was then converted into the station's new control room, which had formerly been located in a separate building across the yard.

Above: *The scene at Willington Quay Co-operative Society's store takes on a Blitz-like appearance after it was gutted by fire in 1957.*

Right: *Willington Quay Co-operative Society's store was completely gutted in February 1957. (Courtesy of* Newcastle Chronicle & Journal*)*

Fires in houses were not unusual occurrences, but one particular fire at Radcliffe near Amble merited particular attention. On the day in question a Mr W. Temple of South Broomhill happened to be passing by when he noticed a fire in one of the houses. A ladder was immediately borrowed and the auxiliary fireman entered the first floor, where he found and rescued a sixteen-month-old child. Although the child unfortunately succumbed to the effects of smoke, a special message of thanks was forwarded to him from the Fire Brigades Committee.

The brigade's fire station replacement programme finally gained momentum and by 1957 approval was at last given for the construction of new stations at Seahouses and Belford. Also, new doors were fitted to Wooler station at this time in order to accommodate one of the new Dennis appliances.

In early February 1958 the brigade was on the receiving end of some adverse publicity when accusations were made by the General Secretary of the Fire Brigades' Union regarding the 'misapplication of manpower'. The allegations were that operational officers and men were being permanently employed on non-operational duties among which upholstery, French polishing, storekeeping, plumbing, gardening, painting and electricians' and mechanics' work were specifically mentioned.

One month later the publicity was better: at a ceremony in the Council Chamber on 19 March, the Lord Lieutenant of the county presented, in the name of Her Majesty the Queen, the British Empire Medal for Gallantry to Fireman A. Thompson and the Silver Laurel and Leaf Emblems and Certificates of Commendation to Firemen C.V. Besford, J.T. Breeze and R. Rochester of Morpeth for their heroism and devotion to duty during a fire on 4 September 1957. At 7.47 a.m. hours on that day, the Morpeth contingent were turned out to a railway

Exercise 'Spring Hazard' was held in the north of the county in March 1957. Firemen and Forestry Commission staff take a well-earned breather after making up miles of hose.

These four Morpeth firemen received awards for bravery, earned while attending a blazing trainload of explosives at West Chevington in September 1957. (Courtesy of Fire International*)*

wagon containing heavy ammunition at Chevington station. On arrival the wagon was well alight. Despite the danger from exploding detonators and the possibility of a very serious explosion that might at any time have caused considerable damage to nearby houses and a signal box, the four firemen, under the leadership of Fireman Thompson, successfully discharged jets of water from the top of a raised embankment loading bay less than 50ft from the wagon. During the operation a series of explosions occurred throwing debris a distance of 40ft. The awards were recommended on the grounds that:

(a) those concerned acted with resolution and determination in the knowledge and comprehension of the danger involved;
(b) their actions in the circumstances were over and above the demands of normal duty.

Three special service incidents of note took place in 1958. The first occurred on 17 June at West Ovingham Bridge near Prudhoe railway station, where a caterpillar mechanical shovel over-balanced into a river, throwing the driver into a pool of water about 10ft deep. The accident was seen by workmen from a nearby railway line but before they reached the spot the man had drowned. Police and firemen used grappling irons to recover the body. On 28 June at 10 p.m. a call was received to the East Ord area of Berwick where three boys aged ten, eleven and twelve were marooned in a 14ft-long fishing boat in the middle of the River Tweed, which at this point was 300 yards wide and in full flood. The boys had dropped anchor but it failed to hold and they were drifting towards the sea. With the aid of rocket apparatus a line was fired over to the boat with the intention of the boys using this to haul a heavier rope for attachment to the boat. However, due to the strength of the current and the weight of the heavy lines, the boys were unable to pull them aboard. The boys were then instructed to make fast the rocket line, weigh anchor and allow the boat to drift down with the current whereupon the firemen, wading in waste deep, secured a hold on the boat and the boys were carried ashore. Two of the boys were removed to hospital suffering from shock and exposure. On 18 August, Newburn was called out by the police to a calf that had fallen down a disused mine air shaft at Hedley West Riding Farm, Prudhoe. On arrival, two National Coal Board officials, already there, expressed apprehension about the condition of the shaft: it was old and no one knew what was at the bottom. The calf could not be seen although it could be heard bellowing. By using a 35ft extension ladder as a probe it became apparent that the shaft was somewhere in the region of 40ft deep. With the ladder suspended within the shaft Fireman Gatenby partly climbed and was partly lowered down the shaft. On the first descent some of the crumbling overhang was dislodged but he successfully managed to remove a baulk of timber which was obstructing access to the calf. On Fireman Gatenby's second descent the calf was secured in an improvised sling, whereupon both the animal and the fireman were hauled to the surface. Neither suffered any ill effects from the drama.

A suitable site for Haltwhistle's new fire station had still not been confirmed at this date. Negotiations with British Paints over the previous four years were not proving fruitful, as the company had changed its mind regarding the sale of the site. Another site had been located, but it was subsequently found that the development costs of the site were likely to be extremely high, so this was abandoned and negotiations were begun over another site at Park View.

The site proposed for the new Wooler station in the centre of the town, approved by the County Council in 1956, was this year being used as a car park and bus station for an experimental period of twelve months. After this it was hoped that the question of the site's disposal would be reviewed. Following this experimental period Glendale Council decided to retain the site for use as a car park, so Wooler's new fire station went back to the drawing board.

Haltwhistle firemen were once again faced with a major fire, when the village's Co-operative Store was engulfed by fire in the early morning hours of 8 October. Alerted at 3 a.m. by a call to his home, the sub officer in charge of the unit immediately operated the call bells, summoning the remainder of the crew, and with a total of eight men on the water tender sped to the scene, a mere 200 yards away from the station. On arrival the whole of the building was found to be heavily smoke-logged, indicating that a severe fire was in progress inside. Intense heat prevented the crew from gaining an entry and tackling the seat of the fire. Shortly afterwards an appliance from Hexham arrived and immediately requested a third appliance, from Haydon Bridge. The heat was so intense that efforts to gain entry were abandoned and within seconds the building erupted into flame. The building was soon alight from end to end, and the roof disintegrated. Five main jets were required in an attempt to stop the fire spreading to adjoining shops. By the time dawn broke, the building was just a smouldering shell. According to the chief fire officer, this type of fire was statistically unlikely to be dealt with by purely retained crews more than once in a decade. In some cases this would have been a fair assumption, but in Haltwhistle's case they had already been faced with the large fire at Blenkinsop Castle and, more ironically, within the following decade Haltwhistle's retained crew would be battling against the odds yet again. The next big fire for Haltwhistle would also turn out to be the most costly to date.

The Beehive Stores at Berwick was severely damaged in January 1958 when fire raged through the first floor and roof of the premises.

The blackened remains of Haltwhistle's Co-operative Store, which was burnt out in the early hours of 8 October 1958. (Courtesy of Fire International*)*

At the end of the year Station Officer Norman Smart, the former Chief Officer of Newburn Urban District Council Fire Brigade, retired after completing thirty years of service, all at Newburn. His son, Norman junior, who had already enrolled in the brigade, would carry on his memory. He continued until his retirement in 1974 as a sub officer at Gosforth.

The brigade still included some of the temporary former wartime firemen on the strength, although it had been hoped, at some time during the brigade's formative years, to introduce a day manning system at Alnwick, Berwick, Hexham and Morpeth stations which required fewer men to operate, and when implemented would see the end of the temporary firemen. It had not been possible to implement the day manning system up to this time because none of the stations had associated housing attached to them or nearby. At Alnwick, a step in the right direction was made, as houses had been constructed in advance of the station. For these reasons the temporary firemen had been kept on to cover the additional manning requirements. The FBU was vehemently against the day manning proposals, so it became increasingly clear that it was now necessary to replace the temporary men, as they resigned, with permanent men. The construction of the new fire station at Alnwick was imminent, and tenders for its erection ready to be sent out in November. The new stations at Bellingham and Seahouses were well under construction and nearing completion and were both operational in 1960. Home Office approval for the erection of drill towers at the two sites was deferred until 1962. At last the brigade was seeing some results from its many years of negotiations and discussions in setting out to achieve continual improvement. Problems still occurred at Haydon Bridge regarding the acquisition of a suitable site, but one was eventually found in California Gardens.

Newburn's former chief officer, Norman Smart, is seen here working the trailer pump at Newburn in front of the Home Office Inspectorate. He retired at the end of 1958 after thirty years of service.

In 1959 a tragic accident occurred within the brigade. Sub Officer George Gladstone, aged forty-six, of Wallsend Fire Station was fatally injured while engaged in firefighting at Willington Farm, Churchill Street, Wallsend on 22 March. He was in charge of a relief crew that had been assigned to finish off clearing up following a fire in an outbuilding. In order to remove smouldering roof timbers the sub officer, who had been in the service since 1939, was standing in the roof valley between the main range of buildings and the building which had been on fire, and was working his way along the guttering when he fell a distance of about 12ft. From investigations following the accident it appeared that the timber beam supporting the lead guttering had been badly affected by dry rot and as he fell, other parts of the roof trussing which had been affected by the fire collapsed and struck his head, inflicting the fatal injuries. This unfortunate event has been the only peacetime fatality suffered by a county fireman, and it is sincerely hoped that it is the last.

Good news came to the firemen in August 1959 when a 56-hour week duty system was introduced in place of the 60-hour week system at the full-time stations at Ashington, Blyth, Gosforth, Newburn, Wallsend and Whitley Bay. This reduction meant that the full-time establishment had to be increased by thirty-three new additions. Less fortunate was the retained establishment. At the same meeting it was determined that the establishment at each of these stations was to be reduced from twenty men to twelve.

Newcastle & Gateshead Joint Fire Service's fireboat *Francis*, berthed at Wincomblee in Walker, for which Northumberland County Council contributed some of the running costs, was declared obsolete and beyond economical repair this year, and was withdrawn from service. No longer considered as an operational necessity, the vessel was not to be replaced and negotiations now commenced between the county and South Shields Fire Brigade regarding an agreement on favourable terms for the use of that brigade's fireboat.

The fact that a fire officer lost his life whilst undertaking damping down operations at this farm outbuilding at Wallsend amply demonstrates the risks that are inherent in the work of the fire brigade.

Newcastle's fireboat Francis, *which was part-funded by Northumberland and the government, was withdrawn in 1958, prompting arrangements to be made with South Shields Fire Brigade for use of their fireboat at riverside incidents.*

All of the retained fire appliances had radios fitted in 1960, considerably improving the efficiency of the brigade in the more remote areas of the county. Now all of the brigade's appliances were equipped with two-way radios. With one exception, the retained stations also all had one of the new Rolls-Royce Dennis water tenders, the exception being Allendale, where the fire station could not accommodate one and where alterations on the restricted site were not feasible (although this would be disputed later). In the meantime, the new appliance was put into the reserve fleet operating from Ashington until their new Commer arrived.

Chief Fire Officer Muir participated in a major Civil Defence exercise in April, 'Exercise Hotspur', where he directed a convoy of AFS appliances from Northumberland to a predetermined destination at Middleton in the Midlothian District of Scotland. The convoy consisted of a mobile column of fifty-seven assorted vehicles drawn from the AFS and Civil Defence, together with 226 personnel. Mobile columns of this magnitude were devised to supply large numbers of resources that would be needed in cases of nuclear attack on the British mainland, and this exercise was testing those kinds of procedures. The travelling time for the 121-mile journey was six hours and many valuable lessons were learned during the proceedings. In the chief officer's report following the event it was remarked that the general consensus was that mobile columns were too unwieldy for convoy exercises. When in close order at the assembly point the vehicles covered a mile of road. While en route, the vehicles were staggered over more than three miles of road. Some criticism was levelled at slower vehicles in the convoy causing untoward separation, notably the large hose layers and personnel carriers which were underpowered, requiring lower gears for even slight inclines. The speed in some instances was little more than walking pace, hence the time taken to travel to Midlothian.

There are thirty-four vehicles in this photograph, almost half of the seventy-five-vehicle convoy of 'Exercise Hotspur'. When under way the convoy stretched out for three miles.

Three more emergency special service calls occurred in 1960 that unfortunately resulted in tragedy. The first occurred at Newburn on 1 July when a young boy was drowned in a brickyard pond. Leading Fireman Mathew Cooley entered the pond assisted by other members of the crew and located the body by feeling around with his bare feet. He then dived under the water, which was about 9ft deep, and brought the body back to the bank where artificial respiration was applied but without success.

The second incident occurred on 26 August in the River Wansbeck at Morpeth, where a young boy had been swept away by the fast flowing current of the river, later being found on a rocky ledge. Firemen from Morpeth station were engaged in the search for two days. When dragging operations failed, Fireman O.M. Thompson, an underwater Aqualung expert, conducted an underwater search using snorkel equipment, and was eventually successful in locating the unfortunate child.

Late in the year, on 4 November at 5 p.m., the brigade was called to a rail crash at West Sleekburn Crossing. Here, two mineral trains had collided at a rail crossing, trapping the driver and fireman of one of the engines, which had overturned. On the arrival of the fire brigade, it was established that two locomotive staff were missing, but it was difficult to confirm this because of the clouds of steam issuing from the wounded locomotives. A railway colleague of the two missing men, on finishing his shift, swiftly came to the location, valiantly entered the cab and diverted the flow of steam, enabling more concerted rescue efforts to commence. After five hours of arduous work and strenuous attempts to rescue the driver and fireman, in conjunction with railway lifting gear, both of the crewmen were unfortunately found to be beyond resuscitation.

The numbers of fire calls continued to increase and this year the brigade attended a record number of calls. In one particular three-month period, 1,091 calls were received, three times greater than average and more than double the previous highest total, in 1949. In one 24-hour period no fewer than fifty-eight calls were received. Many of the appliances were rerouted to other fires by radio, which amply demonstrated the value of brigade-wide radio communication.

The first completely new fire station site was considered this year following the County Planning Committee's proposals for the development of a new town at Cramlington. Massive housing and industrial complexes were proposed for the region and existing fire stations could not have provided the required standards of fire cover for such a large expansion. The area at the time was covered predominantly by appliances from Blyth, with Gosforth providing the second appliance. A new station and an increase in the establishment seemed the only sensible course of action.

Whitley Bay crews undertake the laborious task of damping down smouldering straw at Earsdon Grange Farm. Note the fog applicator on the extreme left.

CHAPTER 3

A NEW DECADE

The brigade was now settling down to some sort of normality. The earlier unsuitable fire stations were now steadily being replaced and the Ashington problem had been rectified temporarily, but complications would still come the brigade's way for some time yet. In May 1960 the council was informed by the proprietors of the Royalty cinema at Gosforth, on whose premises the central workshops had been situated since 1948, that formal notice was being given for the fire service to quit the site. This was extremely galling news and an urgent search was promptly made for alternative suitable premises. The only reasonable premises that could be found at such short notice was an old balloon hangar at a largely disused Royal Air Force depot at Long Benton on the northern outskirts of Newcastle. Negotiations were immediately begun to acquire the site on a short-term basis to bridge the gap until the new headquarters complex at Morpeth was completed. These negotiations were not, however, pursued as a large garage deemed to be eminently more suitable for the workshops became available at Wallsend, and efforts were concentrated on acquiring this. A suitable site for a new Haltwhistle fire station was sealed this year and tenders sought for its construction. Also a site for a new Ashington fire station was secured. At Blyth, a house adjoining the fire station came up for sale and negotiations were started, subject of course to the usual Home Office approval for the house to be purchased, for additional dormitory and mess accommodation to improve the cramped conditions that existed at Blyth.

Throughout the previous decade, Muir's experiments with water supplies in remote areas continued apace when time permitted. Having tried various types of hose, such as plastic and plywood piping, his thoughts turned to adapting standard firefighting delivery hose for use in the forestry regions of the county. The introduction of the new AFS standard appliances with their supplies of six-inch hose was a comforting assurance but these appliances and the manpower for them was not always readily available, so his continued experiments centred on the development of multi-jet hose – Muir's 'holey hose', as it became known. This novel invention consisted of standard lengths of delivery hose fitted with individual small nylon nozzles along the length. The hose would be connected to an appropriate water supply and when laid in a forest ride, would provide an effective water curtain. Much experimentation was done with the hose in a variety of conditions and many exercises were undertaken to test and develop the effectiveness of this type of hose.

The principal role of the firefighter is the preservation of life, and it is always a sad event when circumstances outside the control of the fire service result in loss of life from fire. Two children aged eighteen months tragically lost their lives in a fire at their home at Rocket Way, Forest Hall, and a child of fourteen died in hospital following a house fire at Willington Quay.

Union Street, Blyth, in 1962 showing their brace of Commer appliances.

Multi-jet hose on test at Tranwell, Morpeth in 1962. Morpeth's hose carrier is in the background.

Two other children were successfully rescued in the latter incident by a member of the public before the arrival of the fire brigade. Later on in the year an even greater tragedy occurred. In June, a house fire in Alnwick caused the deaths of four brothers, all under the age of six, and of a neighbour who had tried to rescue them. Such was the intensity of this fire that when the brigade arrived it was impossible to enter the terraced property and it was not until a jet from a hydrant was brought to bear on the ground floor of the house, in conjunction with a hose reel jet through a first floor bedroom window, that the fire was eventually brought sufficiently under control to allow entry into the first floor bedroom where the children were, together with the man who had made a gallant attempt to rescue them. Another neighbour who had attempted a rescue collapsed and had to be removed to hospital where he was treated for serious burns. The cause of the fire was never ascertained but its origin was believed to have been in the region of the fireplace.

Another Commer Miles water tender was delivered in 1960 and assigned to Alnwick, leaving only two more to come – one for Berwick and an additional one for the new Ashington fire station – making a total of ten Commer water tenders and nine pump escapes. The Ashington appliance was ordered from Victor Healey of Churchill Road, Leckhampton, Gloucestershire. The original Miles Company had been incorporated into Dennis Ltd, and Healey Coachbuilders was set up by former Miles engineers. The design of the Ashington appliance was almost identical to the original deliveries. The brigade now had a modern, up-to-date, standardised fleet of appliances with only a few of the former NFS appliances still on the strength, mainly for use in secondary roles. Allendale was still attired with a towing vehicle, as the Rolls-Dennis earmarked for that location was operating at the temporary Ashington station. New equipment ordered

Haltwhistle's Dennis appliance in the position it ended up in after careering through a wall on the Military Road near Chollerford in January 1961.

this year included two Coventry Climax featherweight pumps for evaluating the suitability of mounting them onto the water tenders in place of the wartime Morris-Sigmund pumps.

Accidents occasionally occur to fire appliances, as happens with all vehicles, and in January 1961 the first of the Rolls-Dennis machines, from Haltwhistle, was severely damaged in a road accident when it left the road, careered through a drystone wall and ended up on its side in the middle of a field. It was being driven by a member of the workshop personnel to the transport workshops at Gosforth. The accident, on the Military Road near Chollerford, resulted in the driver being temporarily knocked out in the impact. He was helped to a nearby cottage where an ambulance was called and although suffering from broken ribs and a suspected fractured jaw he was able to make a complete recovery. As for the appliance, it was extensively damaged in the crash and had to be returned to the manufacturer for a total rebuild, after which it was reassigned to Haltwhistle, where it continued to give valuable service to the community. It was eventually withdrawn in 1976 and sold to an industrial brigade at Dudley near Cramlington, where it gave several more years of service.

Another nine of the county's firemen attended the Durham training school in July and once again a Northumberland recruit, D. Bell from Wallsend, was awarded the silver axe for the best recruit.

The original Austin A40 utility vans that were assigned to each full-time station were becoming due for replacement by this time, and the Commer Cob van was the one selected as the replacement. As well as being used for general duties, these vehicles were also the mounts of the station officers, who responded from home at nights and weekends. The original Austins were never fitted with visible or audible warning systems but did feature two-way radios.

Stunned residents from Kenton Road look on as firemen from Gosforth clear up after ten flats were burned out in an early morning blaze.

Withdrawal of the Austin A40 utility vans began in 1961. This one was the steed of Station Officer Frank Davis of Wallsend. (Courtesy of Ian Moore)

By February a site for Haydon Bridge's new fire station was secured, approval for new stations at Haltwhistle and Ashington was passed and the erection of drill towers at Seahouses and Belford stations finally occurred. The featherweight pumps ordered in 1960 for evaluation met the needs of the brigade admirably, prompting the chief fire officer and the brigade's transport officer to travel down to Gloucestershire, the birthplace of the brigade's standard water tenders, to discuss the most suitable form of modification of the fleet to accommodate the new pumps. The water tenders had been originally equipped with Morris Sigmund pumps that dated from 1938. One was mounted inboard but due to the combined weight and unwieldy dimensions, the other had to be towed. Following long discussions, it was agreed that a prototype adaptation be carried out, which provided for an enclosure of the pumps by means of an additional roller shutter at the rear. At a quoted cost of £300, one of the latest water tenders in the fleet, that from Alnwick, was dispatched to Gloucestershire for conversion. The conversion proved successful and greatly improved the efficiency of the appliance. Both of the pumps could be started from the appliance's electrical system and could be easily removed and transported to a convenient water supply. One by one the entire fleet of Miles water tenders was converted to this configuration, which meant the withdrawal of most of the trailer pumps.

Regarding the continual fire station replacement programme, further problems occurred in 1961 when the British Red Cross Society revealed that following the termination of the requisition agreement at Hexham, due to end on 31 December, they would be unable to enter into further arrangements for the brigade to continue to occupy part of the house. They were, however, able to compromise and agreed to temporary accommodation being erected in the grounds next to the appliance garage until a new station could be erected on an alternative site.

A rear view of Alnwick's water tender after conversion, showing the new body extension.

Alnwick's water tender, the first to undergo alterations to the rear bodywork, is pictured on test shortly after completion. The right-hand pump is connected to the water tank by a short piece of soft suction. The lightweight pumps were later altered so that the deliveries faced rearwards.

Six more recruits were dispatched to the regional training school at Durham at the beginning of 1961, and at the March passing out parade Fireman R. Atkinson won the coveted silver axe.

The risks posed to firefighters during the course of their duties is widely acknowledged and this fact was well demonstrated in Northumberland when in July a retained fireman from Blyth fell 30ft from the roof of a power station, sustaining severe injuries including fractures to the spine, pelvis and both ankles. Although making a reasonably successful recovery, the long-term affects were such that the man was declared unfit to continue working for the fire brigade, and he was medically retired, on pension.

The new Alnwick fire station became operational on 14 March, the first full-time station to be completed by the county council. Three appliances were based there: a pump escape, a water tender and hose/personnel carrier, all dual-manned by both full-time and retained personnel. The construction of the new Haltwhistle station was well under way and a site was obtained for Wooler's new station. At Blyth negotiations continued regarding the purchase of a neighbouring council house at No.10 Oxford Street for use as additional accommodation.

Northumberland's countryside has always been deemed a suitable training area for fighter and bomber aircraft of the Royal Air Force and other allied air forces, and until the 1970s there were two active military aerodromes in the county – Ouston on the Military Road near Heddon on the Wall, and Acklington on the Northumberland coast, which later became the site of a prison. Attendances at crashed or disabled aircraft were unfortunately relatively common and in 1962 there were three responses to serious aircraft crashes. On 8 May a pilot lost his life when his aircraft crashed at Cheevey Farm, Acklington, and the very next day another aircraft came to grief near Linton. Fortunately the pilot safely ejected from the stricken aircraft. Later in the year,

Alnwick's new fire station became operational on 14 March 1962, the first new full-time station in the brigade. Housed therein were two Commer pumps and a Karrier hose carrier.

in September, two Hunting Jet provost trainers collided in mid-air near their base at Ouston, resulting in the death of both pilots.

Gosforth was again at the forefront of the brigade's activities in 1962 when the station was called out to one of the biggest fires in its home territory. Called at 3.30 a.m. on 3 August, the pump escape was swiftly dispatched to Station Road, Forest Hall, where numerous calls suggested that the Embassy Ballroom was well alight. On arrival this was found indeed to be the case and not only was the building engulfed in flames but so was a 60-yard block of adjoining shops. Explosions hurled the frontage of the building across the road, fracturing a gas main in the process and setting off a second explosion which blew the back of the building out. This hurled debris onto a house in Northumberland Avenue. Despite reinforcements from other county stations and appliances from neighbouring Newcastle & Gateshead Joint Fire Service, dawn broke to reveal a smouldering heap of burning rubble. The ballroom was no more. At the request of the local council the remains of the once imposing structure were demolished by Civil Defence staff, together with a rescue team from Prudhoe. This operation led to the formation of a permanent Civil Defence staff rescue team that could be mobilised in similar peacetime incidents. Just over two months later, on 8 December, Gosforth's appliances were in attendance at another major blaze. This time it was at High Gosforth Park, where the grandstand was on fire. Most of the imposing structure was wrecked in the fire, together with the Silver Ring Bar that had been built only the previous year. The flames spread rapidly due to strong winds, giving the men a hard job in preventing the fire from spreading to the caretaker's house and the banqueting hall. Six fire crews, including some from Newcastle, under the leadership of Divisional Officer Harkins, eventually brought the blaze under control. This incident was the fourth at the Park in

The Embassy Ballroom at Forest Hall was destroyed in an early morning blaze. Crews from all over south Northumberland and Newcastle attended. (Courtesy of Newcastle Chronicle & Journal*)*

The morning after and fire crews are still damping down smouldering hotspots. Forest Hall's most prominent building was reduced to a pile of rubble.

the previous twelve months. In May a fire and three explosions destroyed the tearoom on the south side of the racecourse. While engaged in fire fighting, Station Officer Sewell narrowly escaped injury from an exploding gas cylinder. As the fire progressed, two further explosions occurred in quick succession. The resultant fires set fire to grassland on the opposite side of the road, necessitating a further appliance being deployed to fight this fire. Upon being interviewed by the press about the fire, Chief Fire Officer Muir, shaking his head in dismay stated, 'It was doomed before we arrived.' Grandstands in Gosforth did not meet with much success, for the first one, built on the appropriately named Grandstand Road, had burned to the ground earlier in the century and had been replaced by an aircraft factory, which burned to the ground in 1921. Another grandstand was constructed at High Gosforth Park and this was burned to the ground in 1915 when occupied by the military.

The early part of March 1963 proved a busy time for Morpeth, when the brigade played a major role in alleviating distress caused by severe flooding of the River Wansbeck after heavy rains. During the early stages of the flooding, crews were engaged in rescue and evacuation measures using fire service vehicles and inflatable rafts. Later they were called upon to carry out pumping operations and assist with the clearance of sludge and debris. The brigade was in action constantly from Thursday 7 March, when the floods began, until the following Tuesday.

Much to the surprise of the council, an objection was raised by Allendale Parish Council and Hexham Rural District Council this year regarding the erection, 'at prohibitive cost', of a new fire station on the previously acquired site at Forstersteads. The Parish Council took the view that the existing station at the rear of the Golden Lion Hotel was conveniently situated and could have been easily adapted at a fraction of the cost of a new building to hold a bigger and more modern fire engine, and that the proposed new station would not add to the efficiency of an already efficient firefighting service. Invited to a meeting with representatives of the rural district council, Chief Fire Officer Muir informed them of the situation, explaining that the existing former NFS station had always been regarded as a temporary expedient. It was still equipped with a wartime towing vehicle and trailer pump because the building, despite every effort to improve it, was not large enough to accommodate a modern fire engine and could not be extended to do so. A modern fire engine had already been delivered for assignment to Allendale but was being used as a reserve until the proposed new station was built in the following year. As far as efficiency was concerned, the chief explained that the new station was less than a quarter of a mile away from the present one and, as the retained men who manned it were recruited locally, the new site was probably further away for some but nearer for others. In summary, it was explained that the Fire Brigades Committee remained satisfied that the proposals for Allendale were necessary and desirable in the interests of providing efficient and adequate cover for the area.

There were no such problems with Ashington's new fire station. Morpeth's MP, Mr Owen, formally opened this on Saturday 7 September 1963. It was manned by full-time and retained personnel and initially equipped with a brand new Commer water tender, the last one to be purchased new by the brigade, and what was to be Allendale's water tender, one of the Dennis F8 appliances. A new pump escape was under construction for delivery the following year. This appliance would be the last Commer to be bought from new but not the last for the fleet as two second-hand ones were acquired some years later. The delivery of the penultimate Commers saw the disposal of the last two prewar appliances, both Leyland limousine motor pumps. The former Blyth appliance was sold to Newcastle & Gateshead Joint Fire Service, where it was needed as a spares source to keep their fleet of five similar appliances operational. The former Newburn UDC Leyland was sold to T. & S. Anderson's of Stamfordham Road, Newcastle, where it was

Ashington's new fire station, opened in 1963, was an unforeseen addition to the establishment following the National Coal Board's withdrawal of fire protection for the area.

This former Newburn Leyland motor pump dating from 1937 was the last of the prewar fire engines to serve the county. It was twenty-six years old when sold in 1963.

converted into a recovery vehicle for the owner's coach company. Both appliances had given over twenty-five years of service.

The year ended on a tragic note with the loss, on 16 December, of a six-week-old baby who died after being removed, apparently unharmed, from a smoke-filled room. A further tragedy was the death of a husband and wife aged eighty-five and ninety-five years, who succumbed in their home on Christmas Day.

The brigade's last multi-purpose pump, now redesignated as a pump escape, ordered in March 1963, was delivered in March 1964 for the new Ashington fire station. This appliance, bodied by Victor Healey Ltd, was the final Commer and the last pump escape to be purchased by the brigade. Unlike the previous Commers it came with an updated front-end assembly. In fact, with the standardised fleet that now existed there were no more new appliances for the next eight years, although some second-hand machines were bought. The oldest appliance in the fleet was now approaching fourteen years of age and getting near to the time when spares would become increasingly scarce.

Pending the completion of the new headquarters, complex consideration was given to relocating the transport workshops to Ashington fire station using the AFS garages at the rear. The owners of the Royalty Cinema at Gosforth were still intent on getting rid of the brigade workshop, having been very patient since the subject was first broached in 1954. Having been under notice to quit since 1960, and despite various sites being viewed, nothing suitable had

The last new Commer and the last pump escape to be delivered to Northumberland was ATY 401B, pictured at Morpeth in 1972. It operated from Ashington and was transferred to Tyne and Wear Metropolitan Fire Brigade in 1974.

been found to replace the building. As a compromise, it was agreed that the fire service would continue to use the site for a further eighteen months, at a vastly increased rent and with an undertaking that when eventually vacated, the council would demolish the building and return the site to a car park. Meanwhile progress was made towards the construction of the new headquarters complex at Morpeth, with tenders already having been agreed; the same applied for the proposed new stations at Prudhoe and Allendale.

Assistant Chief Fire Officer Taylor retired from the brigade on 6 May after thirty years in the fire service, twenty of them in Northumberland, in order to take up an appointment as chief instructor at the Home Office Fire Service Training Centre, Moreton-in-Marsh, Gloucestershire. His successor was Joseph Henshaw, recruited from the South Eastern Area Fire Brigade, Edinburgh. Mr Henshaw joined the fire brigade in 1947 after leaving the Forces and was promoted successively to the rank of divisional officer in Edinburgh, following a period of secondment as an instructor at the Fire Service College.

At this time many of the brigade's calls were assistance calls to fires in other areas. In the previous year a total of 454 calls were attended in neighbouring brigade areas. Most of these calls were in Newcastle & Gateshead Joint Fire Service's area, involving stations at Newburn, Wallsend and Gosforth, whose areas surrounded the city. Certain parts of Gosforth's turnout area became notorious for heavy fire activity, especially Fawdon, Kenton, Blakelaw and Cowgate, and continued to be so for many years. Gosforth's crews were frequently engaged in fires in these areas until relieved by appliances from Newcastle & Gateshead Joint Fire Service.

On the night of 10 December 1964, Gosforth was fully committed for several hours assisting Newcastle at the city's biggest blaze since the war. Alerted by an automatic alarm that activated at 7.30 p.m., the pump escape was turned out to Winthrop's Laboratories, Edgefield Avenue, Fawdon, a large chemical plant. Although in Newcastle's area, this complex posed a significant risk and, with Gosforth being the nearest fire station, an appliance from here was assigned as part of the first attendance. The premises frequently needed the attendance of the fire service for small fires and false alarms, and this call appeared to be no different until the machine with Sub Officer Jack Stephenson and his crew of three rounded the corner into Edgefield Avenue. Large volumes of smoke and angry red flame were noted emitting from the roof of a large single-storey goods warehouse. The entire building was well alight. With only four men, the crew had a hard task in getting jets and hydrants to work to try to prevent the fire spreading to some exposed oil tanks. Pumps were made up to four as the men held their ground until supplemented by the arrival of two pumps from Newcastle's West Road fire station. Eventually a total of eight pumps were required to extinguish the fire, but this was not achieved before the entire north wall of the building fell inwards following the collapse of the roof. Gosforth's appliance was in attendance for five hours. Fate is a strange thing, and almost one year later, at midnight on 15 November 1965, Gosforth were again turned out to Winthrop's Laboratories for an automatic alarm activation. Sub Officer Wilf Thompson was in charge on this occasion and once again, upon rounding Edgefield

The north wall at the first Winthrop's Laboratories fire. The style of helmets denotes that the two lone firemen are from Northumberland County. (Courtesy of Newcastle Chronicle & Journal*)*

Avenue, the crew was greeted by large volumes of smoke and flame emitting from the recently rebuilt warehouse. Almost the same number of men and appliances were required to control this second conflagration and the circumstances were so similar that it was like putting the clock back eleven months. Two fires of this magnitude in so short a time were too much of a coincidence and a youth was later charged with maliciously starting the blazes.

During the mid-morning of 16 July 1965, six county pumps from Whitley Bay, Wallsend and Gosforth together with others from Newcastle were called in to assist the Tynemouth County Borough Fire Brigade, which was battling a major fire at the Tyne Brand food processing and canning factory on Brewers Bank near the Fish Quay, North Shields. Such was the magnitude of the fire that the flames could be seen by the Gosforth men racing to the scene when they were at Four Lane Ends, Benton, some six miles away. The five-storey building was completely gutted in the blaze and fourteen main jets and one turntable ladder monitor had to be brought into operation before this fire was brought under control. An abundance of water from the nearby River Tyne proved a useful facility in the extinction of this fire, the borough's biggest in fifteen years.

Chief Fire Officer Muir's experiments with forest fire extinction in the Kielder and Redesdale areas continued unabated and it was now thought appropriate to place an order for twenty 75ft lengths of multi-jet hose for use at forest fires. It was also proposed to assign some of the hose to various fire stations to evaluate its uses as general-purpose hose.

Wallsend's water tender had every inlet and delivery in use, relaying water to other appliances at the Tyne Brand factory, North Shields in July 1965. (Courtesy of Ian Moore)

Construction of the new Prudhoe fire station, on a site that also contained the county council's ambulance station, began in 1965, but was marred by the death of a forty-year-old workman on the site, who had been overcome by fumes while working in the tank chamber of a petrol pump and was found to be dead when extricated. The station became operational on 21 September 1965. Negotiations began for a site for Berwick's new station and a suitable site was found for Newburn's new station. Construction of the latter was scheduled to begin in 1966, but was deferred as it was thought prudent to acquire the Throckley site first if at all possible and then commence construction at a later date. Approval for the acquisition of a site for a new fire station at Station Road, opposite Mullen Road, in Wallsend, gained approval in December, but the planned expansion at Blyth by the incorporation of adjoining houses was abandoned. Current developments at Wallsend and the pattern of future developments in the town now prompted the council to seek a new site on the perimeter of the borough. The erection of Haydon Bridge's new fire station continued and the premises were officially occupied on 16 November.

The firemen's working week was reduced this year from fifty-six hours to forty-eight hours at all of the full-time stations. This required an increase in the brigade's establishment of thirty-three full-time men. Because of the alleged inability to recruit men of the required standard in sufficient numbers, the recruitment was phased in over a twelve-month period.

A fine display of the multi-jet hose in action in a forest ride at Kielder in 1964.

New warning systems made their appearance in the county this year, when most appliances, with the exception of the six hose carriers and the AFS vehicles, started to be fitted with two-tone air horns, which superseded the traditional fire bell that had warned people of the approach of the fire engine since the turn of the century. The alternating tone devices were fitted behind the front grills of the Commers and Dennises and, to ensure that the electric fire bell became obsolete, it was disconnected and the air horns wired to the bell switch. The hand bell, however, remained for use in cases of the air horns becoming defective. Six months later, rotating blue beacons made an appearance on the brigade's appliances. The pump escapes were fitted with a single one and the water tenders with two. The station officers' utility vans were also fitted with blue lights, but not air horns. For some reason, probably cost, it was deemed not necessary to fit these devices onto the hose carriers. Before the advent of the all-round vision revolving blue lights, the appliances relied on twin amber-coloured blinker lights mounted above the windscreen. The warning aspect of these lights was therefore limited, restricted to objects in front of the vehicles.

Opposite above: *Gosforth fire station had occupied this site since 1902, the appliances entering the Great North Road through an archway of the Council Chambers. The base of the railings shows where the original roadway was before it was lowered to allow sufficient clearance for the pump escape.*

Opposite below: *Haydon Bridge fire station was opened in November 1965. The appliance is the reserve Commer-Whitson water tender, formerly from Alnwick.*

CHAPTER 4

NEW HEADQUARTERS

As 1966 approached, construction of the new headquarters was well under way, and because of the impending termination of tenancies at Roseworth and the Royalty at Gosforth, the new buildings were occupied promptly when they were completed. The fire station staff at Morpeth occupied the site and commenced operations on 4 February, with the administration staff from Gosforth moving in some ten days later. It had taken eighteen years to come to fruition. The brigade now boasted a modern, standardised fleet of appliances and, as for the premises, the building plans were gradually seeing the obsolete fire stations replaced.

The brigade's appliances were being mobilised to an increasing number of calls to assist the ambulance service with the removal of casualties at road accidents and industrial accidents, and in view of this, ten hydraulic rescue sets, one for each full-time station, were purchased. The 'Flexi-Force' portable hydraulic emergency equipment, supplied by Epco Ltd of Leeds, was of

The main building at the new Morpeth headquarters complex was occupied in February 1966 and contained the administration offices, brigade control and fire station.

Above: *These 'fire belles' are obviously very pleased with the facilities of the new control room at Morpeth.*

Opposite above: *The new 'flexi-force' equipment was used to good effect at this Seaton Burn road accident in 1967.*

Opposite below: *The tangled remains of Smith & Walton's paint factory, Haltwhistle, in 1966. This was the scene of Northumberland's costliest fire to date.*

6–8-ton capacity and featured a comprehensive range of adapters, enabling constant pressure to be applied to impacted vehicle components, such as foot pedals and steering columns. The compact, hand operated kit, weighing just 98lb, was contained in a steel box that was usually stored in a convenient place in the appliance room so that it could be placed on any of the appliances as required.

On 2 June Haltwhistle's firemen attended their biggest fire to date when flames engulfed the plant of the local paint and varnish manufacturer, Smith & Walton (Hadrian Paints) Ltd. The fire started in the early hours of the morning after flammable liquid leaked onto an exposed gas flame. The town's sole appliance was met on arrival by a severe fire which eventually required the attendance of ten pumps, including two from Newcastle & Gateshead and one from Cumbria, before the conflagration was brought under control. Three plant operatives had to run for their lives as exploding tins of paint were violently propelled around the site. These 'bombs', together with flames 100ft high, hampered the firemen's attempts to control the blaze, but gallant

Unknown to these AFS men, their services – and indeed the organisation – were running out of time.

work prevented the flames from reaching storage tanks of white spirit, fuel oil and linseed oil. The financial cost of this fire amounted to almost £500,000, and was the county's biggest single fire loss to date. Following the fire, the works fire team was supplemented in November 1968 by the acquisition of a Morris-Sigmund trailer pump from the county brigade. The complex was rebuilt and resumed production to remain a major employer in the district, and despite successive takeovers remained in production until its closure was announced in October 2001, with the loss of 100 jobs.

The county's AFS was mobilised in mid-November at the request of the National Coal Board, when a major underground fire at Lynemouth Colliery threatened the future production of coal at the mine. The brigade was first given notice of this fire on the 14th, when they were approached by the Coal Board regarding the use of foam at the fire. Nothing further developed until the 18th, when a request was made for the brigade to assist with pumping water into the pit in quantities and rates which NCB engineers estimated might be enough to isolate the area of fire. This underground fire had been smouldering in an isolated part of the mine workings for two years, but suddenly flared up, forcing the withdrawal of all the miners from the seam.

Seven of the county's AFS Green Goddess emergency pumps were engaged for several days at the Lynemouth Colliery fire. Here the appliances are seen pumping water from the Lyne Burn.

Despite the efforts of twenty-two pumps from the Coal Board and the attendance of rescue brigade units from Ashington, Benwell and Houghton le Spring, the fire burned on. With the assistance of six fire crews from the County Fire Brigade with Green Goddess pumps set into the Lyne Burn, the quantity of water being pumped down the 60ft deep mine was raised to 750,000 gallons an hour and was continued at this rate for several days. The use of the AFS at this incident not only relieved the regular brigade but also provided training for members of the AFS, many of whom provided long hours of duty. The unusual sight of numerous Green Goddess engines lined up with miles of hose laid out provided an interesting site for the locals and no doubt gave the AFS a great deal of publicity. Unknown to anyone at the time, the days of the AFS, and the entire Civil Defence organisation, were numbered, and such a resource would never be available again – or would it?

On 20 December 1966 Gosforth became involved in the rescue of eighteen people from the first floor of an office at Causey Buildings on the High Street. At 9.30 a.m. the crews were met with the sight of numerous people standing at the windows waiting to be rescued as smoke poured from the building. Prior to the brigade's arrival, an intrepid television engineer from one of the offices was able to drop to the ground and with the aid of ladders from his company van managed to start rescuing the trapped people. With a crew of only four the firemen were once again hard pressed to slip the wheeled escape and extension ladder and carry out the remainder of the rescues. Fortunately an off duty Gosforth fireman in an adjacent shop assisted the crew with getting water supplies connected to the machine. The actual fire damage was relatively slight but smoke filling the building and preventing a route of escape via the staircase could have resulted in tragedy but for the television engineer and the prompt attention of the fire brigade.

The riverbank towns of Wallsend and Blyth posed considerable risks for the brigade's fire crews because of the heavy shipbuilding and ship repair industries along the rivers Tyne and Blyth. Attendances to these high-risk areas were common and this was the principal reason why Wallsend fire station had two full-time manned appliances. In fact one of the first major fires attended by the brigade was at Swan Hunter's shipyards, when fire severely damaged the

Causey Buildings on Gosforth High Street, where the fire brigade and a television engineer rescued eighteen people who were trapped on the upper floor. The wheeled escape is pitched to its lowest level.

The ill fated Egton *in dry dock at Wallsend after the fire of January 1967.*

pattern shop and finance offices at the yard. On 30 January 1967, Wallsend was turned out to Swan Hunter's and Wigham Richardson's yard for a reported fire on board the merchant ship *Egton*. The vessel had been dry docked as the result of a grounding incident off Whitby. Oil leaking from the damaged hull ignited and before long flames 50ft high were spreading up the side of the ship, as one fireman was to relate 'just as if it were a cauldron sitting on a fire'. With assistance from Newcastle & Gateshead Joint Fire Service, foam and water jets were quickly deployed and with the dock bottom flooded to several feet the fire was quickly extinguished. The vessel, owned by the now defunct Whitby firm of Headlam & Sons, was something of a jinx. From its place of birth at Sunderland it went immediately into lay-up because of lack of work and after a few years of trading was laid up again at Hartlepool for several years before being towed to Finland for scrapping. The ship had the distinction of being laid up longer than any other British vessel.

At the request of Durham County Fire Brigade, which had invoked district mobilising on behalf of the South Shields County Borough Fire Brigade, Gosforth's pump escape went long distance again when it was dispatched to South Shields, where a major fire was in progress at the premises of Cigarette Components on the Bede Trading Estate. This fire destroyed a two-storey building used for the storage of crêpe paper and concentrated efforts had to be made to prevent the fire spreading to adjoining premises. Gosforth's was once again the furthest travelled appliance out of a total of twenty pumps mobilised to the fire, which was the borough's biggest peacetime fire to date.

Three years had elapsed since any new fire engines had been delivered, and consideration was now given to replacing some of the earlier vehicles. Of the thirty-two appliances in the fleet, twenty-eight had been in use for between ten and seventeen years but because of the high standards of maintenance by the brigade's workshops they were expected to give another five or

This towing vehicle, pictured at Rothbury when in use as a mobile workshop, was withdrawn in 1968. It had the distinction of being the last of the former NFS appliances to be disposed of. (Courtesy of Angus Patterson)

Four firemen were injured, two of them seriously, when Alnwick's water tender crashed on Belford High Street in July 1967 on its way to a farm fire near Lowick. (Courtesy of Photo Centre, Berwick)

six years of operational service. In the meantime, four Ford Thames 15cwt ambulances that were surplus to the Civil Defence were bought for use as auxiliary towing vehicles. One of them was later converted into a stores van. The purchase of these vehicles saw the withdrawal of the last of the wartime NFS appliances, when the remaining three Austin towing vehicles were sent to Tranwell for storage before being sold for scrap. Apart from the first two Commer deliveries of 1950, the brigade's appliance fleet was completely standardised on Miles appliances, facilitating standardised maintenance procedures and familiarity of equipment amongst the brigade's twenty fire stations.

However, tragedy came on the warm summer's evening of 28 July 1967, just after the night duty commenced, when Alnwick's water tender was involved in a serious accident on Belford Main Street. The appliance was en route from Alnwick to a farm fire at Bowsden near Lowick when it left the road after a bend, just opposite Belford police station. The machine went out of control, smashed along the front of an antique shop, across a side street and ended up in the corner of a house. Villagers rushed to the site and with the aid of the police managed to free the injured crewmembers, all of whom had to be transported to hospitals in Newcastle, suffering injuries ranging from head injuries to multiple fractures. Injuries sustained by two of the crew were such that they were unable to return to operational duties and had to retire on medical grounds. Just as unfortunate, the appliance involved was one of the newest in the fleet and the first to have undergone the pump conversion. Damage to the machine was such that it was written off by the insurers, leaving the fleet minus one appliance, as one of the two reserve engines now had to be assigned to Alnwick. Immediate replacement was necessary and in order to maintain standardisation and avoid complicating the future replacement programme, a 1951 Commer/Miles water tender of the type used in Northumberland was purchased second-hand from Gloucestershire Fire Brigade. Before entering service it was sent to Miles Engineering where it underwent the conversion programme to the rear bodywork in accordance with the pattern of the rest of the brigade's water tenders.

Suitable sites for a new Rothbury station were still being sought, and although the site of the present station was eminently suitable, another more appropriate one came to light in December on land owned by the Rothbury Auction Mart, which adjoined the police station. Negotiations for the acquisition of this site proved successful, and arrangements were made for the disposal of the present site and garage buildings back to Rothbury UDC. The lease at Hexham was due to expire in 1971 and, as it was thought that the landowners were unlikely to renew it, alternative sites were urgently required here. An ideal alternative site was located at Corbridge. Aware of their own commitments and anxious to assist the fire brigade, the British Red Cross Society agreed to grant a further three-year extension of the lease. On this basis, the question of a new fire station was once again deferred. Castle Ward RDC was now requesting that consideration be given to establishing units of the fire service and ambulance service in or near Ponteland because of the growing development in the area. The county council, however, was of the opinion that adequate fire cover was being provided by Gosforth and Newburn, both stations being capable of making attendances in the prescribed times. The council doubted whether a review of the standards of fire cover currently provided was called for. More appropriately, the proposed building of Newburn's new station at Throckley would substantially enhance the fire cover in the Ponteland and Darras Hall areas, but bearing in mind that some extension of fire cover might be required in the 1970s, preliminary enquiries were made for selecting a suitable site.

During the mid-1960s a new type of fire engine had been introduced into the country following its development in the United States. Manufactured by Simon Engineering Ltd, and available on a variety of chassis, this 'Simon Snorkel' high-rise hydraulic platform appliance was demonstrated to the brigade in April 1967. This type of appliance, with boom heights ranging

Above: *The replacement for Hexham fire station was becoming increasingly urgent, because the site owners wanted the premises for other purposes. The garages later became the town's ambulance station.*

Left: *Pictured at Morpeth in 1967, this Bedford 'snorkel' appliance was demonstrated to the brigade in April 1967, but none were purchased.*

Opposite: *The last gathering of the counties AFS occurred at Morpeth in March 1968, when the illustrious organisation was officially stood down. The large bay window in the background was where the brigade control was situated.*

from 50ft to 85ft, soon become accepted by many fire brigades throughout the country, but in Northumberland's case no orders were forthcoming. In fact, although there were tentative plans later to purchase a turntable ladder, the lack of tall buildings in the county and the proximity of aerial appliances in Tyne and Wear to the south and Lothian and Borders to the north would have made the acquisition of such an appliance an expensive and perhaps little used luxury. To this day there are no aerial appliances in the county.

The Home Office allocated additional radio frequencies to the emergency services towards the end of 1967, meaning that the hitherto shared system with the police could now be operated independently, to the mutual benefit of both services. The brigade was allocated its own radio channel, with Tynemouth Fire Brigade being linked to the county scheme, as its requirements did not justify an independent scheme. Communications between Tynemouth appliances and their control room was now possible via talk-through facilities with Northumberland's brigade control.

Malicious false alarms, mainly transmitted by children, continued to show an annual increase and in 1967 the brigade attended 274 of these calls. This caused a vast drain on resources, not to mention the risks of delayed responses. So concerned was the Fire Brigades Committee that the chief fire officer was asked to suggest ways in which these calls could be reduced. One method adopted was that of making an approach to local schools and publicising the dangers and adverse effects of these calls.

At the end of the year the government suddenly and without warning revealed that the Civil Defence was being placed on a 'care and maintenance basis' and recruitment and training in these areas was to be suspended. In effect this meant that the Civil Defence Corps and the Auxiliary Fire Service were to be disbanded. Northumberland had always made a huge commitment to its AFS section and the recruitment of volunteers required much finance and

time in maintaining the enthusiasm and motivation of the individuals concerned, even to the extent of establishing the camp at Kielder. Although having been in existence for almost twelve years and never used for the purpose for which it was intended – fortunately – the organisation was a useful supportive resource in civil emergencies, as had been proved not twelve months earlier at Tynemouth.

The early part of 1968 was a busy one for the brigade. On 15 January fifty-one calls were received for assistance in connection with damage to property during a period of gales. On 31 March, in accordance with the previously made announcement, the AFS was formally disbanded. On that day a stand-down parade was held at headquarters, attended by fifty-five members of the service. The chairman of the county council and the chairman of the Fire Brigades Committee addressed the parade and each member was handed a copy of a personal message from Her Majesty the Queen. Copies of this message were also sent by post to those members who were unable to attend the parade. The only premises held exclusively for the AFS were a garage at Bedlington belonging to the UDC and four hutments at Kielder belonging to the Forestry Commission. Except for one hut at Kielder, which was retained for a short while for the continuing training of regular firemen, everything else was returned to the original owners. All of the appliances assigned to the brigade's AFS section were placed in storage to await return to Home Office stores via Tranwell, Morpeth. The Green Goddesses would not be seen on the roads of Northumberland again ... or would they? There was an arrangement whereby fire brigades could purchase surplus equipment that was of use for normal firefighting operations, and to this end the county bought two Bedford emergency pumps, two featherweight pumps, two inflatable dams and one electric blower. The emergency pumps were Bedford four-wheel-drive machines that were assigned to the reserve fleet and proved to be amply suitable for working in the county. Before becoming operational, however, they were loaned to Newcastle

Northumberland County Fire Brigade loaned their two newly acquired Green Goddesses to Newcastle Airport, where they are pictured here, still in the original green livery. (Courtesy Ian Moore)

Airport for six months while the airport authority awaited delivery of a new major crash tender. Upon delivery of the new airport appliance, the two Green Goddesses were returned to the County Fire Brigade fleet, where they operated as brigade reserves still adorned in the original olive green livery. For some time the ungainly engines operated throughout the county with little modification apart from the fitting of radio facilities. They were not even fitted with updated warning systems, the driver having to rely on the front mounted orange blinker lights and hand operated bell to warn oncoming traffic. Eventually they were repainted red and fitted with blue lights and air horns, and with the addition of the county coat of arms the machines ended up looking quite attractive and business-like.

In September the opportunity was taken to acquire a surplus former Civil Defence signals office van. This unit, mounted on a Ford Thames chassis, was modified into a 'Combined Emergency Services Communications Unit'. Available for use also by the ambulance service and police, the vehicle featured VHF radio facilities for all three emergency services. Factors considered in the interior design were those of 'uncomplicated simplicity', and any attempt to add 'gimmickry' of any kind was studiously resisted. Inside the unit there were three separate soundproofed cubicles at the front, each with a VHF radio for one of the emergency services, and at the rear there were three separate telephone systems that could be connected to GPO lines to establish landline communications. In the outside lockers was situated the field telephone apparatus. The machine was stationed at Morpeth and was the first of its type in the county. Unfortunately it did not see much use and after nine years of service it was replaced by a small Ford Transit van, dedicated solely to the fire brigade. Thereafter it was acquired by a preservationist who rallied it as a flat platform lorry, the body no doubt being used as a shed somewhere.

Alnwick's 'new' water tender was now operational and differed from the others in the fleet in having a painted front grille instead of the attractive chromed bars of the original county

Northumberland's combined emergency services control unit was converted from a Civil Defence signals unit. The vehicle had four roof-mounted beacons, two amber and two blue in diagonal corners.

This Alnwick water tender was bought from Gloucestershire to replace one that was written off at Belford. It was instantly recognisable by the red-painted radiator bars.

machines. Following this successful conversion the opportunity was taken to acquire another surplus appliance for modification and attachment to the reserve fleet. Warwickshire County Fire Brigade was the donor of this appliance.

Wallsend's water tender escape came to grief in the summer when it was involved in a collision with a car at the junction of Church Bank and Ropery Lane while on its way to a reported fire at Tyne Timbers Ltd, Willington Quay. A young Newcastle man unfortunately lost his life in the collision and the passenger received facial and head injuries. In the crash the car was pushed several yards but as soon as the vehicles came to a halt the fire engine crew began the desperate battle to try and save the injured car occupants while an ambulance sped to the scene. None of the engine's crew were injured and the 8-ton appliance received only slight damage to the front panels, although this area did require replacement. When the appliance returned to service it reappeared with a modern front assembly, belying the fact that it was the prototype and the oldest of its type in the fleet.

During the annual visit of Her Majesty's Inspector of Fire Services an exercise with a difference was held. Arrangements were made to test the effectiveness of fighting fires at sea and many valuable lessons were learned during the joint exercise with the Royal Air Force and the Royal National Lifeboat Institution. Firemen became airborne for the first time, using a Royal Air Force Whirlwind rescue helicopter to ferry featherweight pumps from headquarters and RAF Acklington to a lifeboat out in the North Sea. The use of helicopters would later be developed further with regard to incidents at Holy Island.

Although originally occupied in part in 1966 it was not until 11 November 1968 that the headquarters complex at Morpeth was formally opened. Mr Merlyn Rees MP, parliamentary

Gosforth's pump escape stops to render assistance at the crash at Ropery Bank, Wallsend. The damaged car is a Ford Cortina. (Courtesy of Ian Moore)

The new transport workshops at Morpeth were a big improvement over the cramped facilities at Gosforth. On the ramps undergoing maintenance are Ashington's Commer Cob utility van, the former Berwick Carmichael water tender and Morpeth's pump escape.

Above: *Acklington's Westland Whirlwind rescue helicopter prepares to set down in the yard at Morpeth.*

Left: *During the new headquarters opening ceremony a hook ladder demonstration, precariously carried out in co-ordination with a musical accompaniment, was rehearsed in full the day before the official opening.*

under-secretary of state, was the dignitary appointed to officiate at the opening ceremony. The invited guests were treated to an elaborate display of firefighting techniques and rescue drills, including a demonstration of scaling the drill tower with hook ladders, accompanied to the sound of music. In contrast to this ancient item of equipment, a rescue was demonstrated using one of the latest innovations in firefighting, when a second Simon Snorkel hydraulic platform demonstrator was loaned by the manufacturers for the display. On this occasion the appliance was an incompletely bodied ERF with 75ft booms. As well as the rescue scenarios, the programme of events included a demonstration of an old hand-drawn manual fire engine in comparison to one of the brigade's up to date Miles appliances, and a road accident demonstration, where an old towing vehicle loaned from Tranwell was righted onto its wheels using Tirfor winching equipment. The impressive range of demonstrations culminated in the appearance of a bright yellow Westland Whirlwind Air–Sea Rescue helicopter which was positioned over the drill tower and, with the aid of a diver lowered down from the aircraft, accomplished a rescue from the roof of the tower by winching the supposed victim into the helicopter.

CHAPTER 5

MUIR RETIRES

Although there were still some fire stations to replace, the official opening of the new headquarters was the culmination of Muir's tenure as Northumberland's first chief fire officer. His retirement was obviously inevitable at some point, and at the beginning of 1969 it was announced that he was to retire on pension from 1 March. He had completed thirty-eight years in firefighting, of which twenty-one had been in the county's service. During his service in Northumberland he had organised the replacement of many of the former NFS fire stations and saw through the construction of the brigade's new headquarters complex. Also, almost the entire appliance fleet had been replaced, making Northumberland one of the most up-to-date fire brigades in the country. Muir had also been largely responsible for the organisation of the firefighting arrangements in the country's most extensive forests at Kielder, and was at the forefront of many developments that had taken place in the important field of fire prevention. He was awarded the Queen's Fire Service Medal in 1960.

There was no doubt that his act would be a hard one to follow. Five prospective applicants applied for the vacant position. These were the existing chief officers of Tynemouth and Cumberland Fire Brigades and the deputy chief officers of Warwickshire, Worcestershire and Northumberland. The successful applicant was Northumberland's Deputy Chief Fire Officer Joseph Henshaw, who took up the post from 1 April 1969. Mr Colin E. Bates from Nottinghamshire County Fire Brigade was appointed deputy chief fire officer. One of the new chief officer's first tasks was a complete review of the brigade; resulting from this was a change from the existing two divisions based at Alnwick and Morpeth to three divisions based at Alnwick, Morpeth and Newburn.

The second month of the new chief officer's tenure saw the brigade called out to its first major disaster when, just after 1.30 a.m. on 7 May, the *Aberdonian* sleeping car express train was derailed just north of Morpeth station. The train had just passed through the station and owing to excessive speed was derailed on a sharp curve that had a mandatory 40mph speed limit. Six passengers and the ticket collector lost their lives and 121 others suffered injuries, with forty-six requiring hospital treatment and nineteen of them being seriously injured. The previously formulated Emergency Plan for Major Disasters was immediately put into effect, resulting in the mobilisation of eleven appliances and sixty-three officers and men, including an emergency tender from Newcastle & Gateshead Joint Fire Service. The scene that greeted the first crews to arrive from Morpeth and Ashington revealed a tangled mass of wreckage with many walking wounded seeking medical attention, and many others trapped in the twisted and overturned carriages. The county's emergency services were commended for their skilful use of equipment and manpower and for the occasional improvisation that enabled all the trapped passengers to be released. Ironically, these skills would be tested again in the future, at the same location.

In 1969 Chief Fire Officer Muir (left) handed over the control of the brigade to his deputy, Joseph Henshaw (to his right), another native of Scotland.

Daylight at the Morpeth train crash revealed the scene of carnage that greeted the emergency services when they first arrived in the early morning hours of 7 May 1969.

On the first day of August a major fire in Newcastle saw the county involved with assisting the Newcastle & Gateshead Joint Fire Service again, when fire ripped through a tyre warehouse at Westgate Road. Both of Gosforth's appliances were mobilised to the fire, the full-time crew at the time manning Berwick's old water tender, complete with trailer pump and still bearing the Berwick name plate on the door, much to the surprise of the hoards of bystanders.

The Fawdon and North Kenton areas of Newcastle continued to be the scene of very heavy fire activity involving fires started maliciously by children, especially during the summer and autumn periods when the surrounding corn fields had dried out. Almost every night crews from Gosforth and Newcastle were in attendance, especially in the Dorrington Road and Fawdon Lane areas. On one night in particular, Gosforth made four consecutive turnouts to Dorrington Road. This heavy fire activity continued well into the 1970s and gained some publicity in the local press, when Tyne and Wear Fire Brigade publicised its concern over the drain on resources in these areas. The encroaching development of Kingston Park housing estate resulted in the reduction of these once rural areas that surrounded north Newcastle and a consequent reduction in fire activity.

In August, the popular Whitley Bay night spot, the Sands Club, above the town's bus station, was severely damaged by fire in an early morning blaze. Both Whitley Bay crews were supplemented by a crew from neighbouring Tynemouth Fire Brigade. During the following month classrooms at Bedlington School were razed to the ground in a spectacular evening fire that required eight pumps to bring under control.

In 1965 the GPO had announced changes to the telephone network, notably the introduction of subscriber trunk dialling, which in effect meant the centralisation of fire calls. By 1969 the

The former Berwick Carmichael water tender, complete with trailer pump, arrives at a ten-pump fire at Firestone Tyres, Westgate Road, Newcastle, in August 1969. (Courtesy of Ian Moore)

Whitley Bay crews are still damping down at the Sands Club on Whitley Road after the interior was gutted by fire in August 1969.

Several crews were required at Bedlington Station County Secondary School when fire ravaged the building in September 1969. (Courtesy of Newcastle Chronicle & Journal)

system was in place and all fire calls were now centralised at Morpeth Fire Brigade Control. No longer were calls received at individual fire stations, negating the need to have a permanent man assigned to watchroom duties. At every full-time fire station one man per duty had been detailed to watchroom duties and was responsible for the receipt of fire calls and general enquiries, dispatching the appliance, activating the retained call bells and sirens and then informing control. All messages relayed from control were then entered in the station occurrence book. It was a lonely life for the watchroom attendant on night shift. Sixteen hours with only a one-hour relief for supper meant a long night unless a fire call came in to relieve the monotony. Sleeping in the watch room was not allowed. Under the new system, station alarm bells, retained call-out alarms and even the station lights were operated by remote control. A reduction in manpower by eighteen firemen was achieved through this automation by either natural wastage or retirement.

On the bitterly cold night of 30 November 1969, Newcastle & Gateshead Joint Fire Service were turned out to what would be the biggest peacetime fire in the city. The Callers department store on Northumberland Street was engulfed in flames that threatened to involve neighbouring properties. During the first hour of the fire, fifteen pumps plus several special appliances were progressively ordered to the scene. Six county appliances from Gosforth, Newburn, Wallsend and Whitley Bay attended the fire, together with one from Durham County Fire Brigade, and twenty jets were ultimately directed at the fire before it was brought under control. At no time since have so many Northumberland pumps worked in the city. Ironically, almost two years later, on 9 October 1971, just as the building had been reconstructed, an adjacent partly disused building under renovation was the scene of a ten-pump fire. Once again Northumberland appliances were back in the city, supplying two pumps from Gosforth to aid the Newcastle Brigade.

Six Northumberland pumps were ordered to Caller's department store, Northumberland Street, Newcastle, on 18 November 1969, where Newcastle & Gateshead Fire Service were battling their biggest postwar blaze. Wallsend and Gosforth appliances are lined up awaiting instructions.

August 1969 saw the retirement of one of the most well respected retained fire officers in the history of the brigade. Station Officer Bobby Bolam of Rothbury was hanging up his uniform after thirty years of service in the town. He first joined the brigade as a volunteer fireman, later becoming the captain in charge of the Rothbury Rural District Council Fire Brigade. In 1941 he became a member of the NFS and was incorporated into the County Brigade in 1948. He was awarded the Long Service and Good Conduct Medal in 1960 and the British Empire Medal in 1962. He was apparently quite an inventive force and when the brigade announced the introduction of fog applicators in the 1960s, he was able to produce one that he had devised and made several years before! In accepting his retirement, the chief fire officer publicly stated that 'by virtue of constant service, intimate knowledge and technical ability, personality and unflagging enthusiasm Mr Bolam has been a driving force at Rothbury and he has contributed to the efficiency and representation of the brigade in unique measures. I shall be very sorry to lose his services.' A fine accolade for one of the part-timers. This man was one of the last retained officers to hold the rank of station officer, a position inherited from the former prewar and National Fire Service days.

In March 1970 Widdrington Social Club was severely damaged by fire. The club's patrons had not long been in their homes enjoying their Sunday lunches when smoke was noticed coming from the roof of the building. By the time the first appliance arrived the roof was heavily on fire. With the use of breathing apparatus, the seat of the fire was located and quickly knocked down, but not before the interior had sustained severe damage. Five pumps from Ashington, Morpeth, Blyth, Alnwick and Amble attended this fire. In the same month a single-storey upholstery manufacturers at Planet Place, Killingworth, was severely damaged by fire. The burning polyurethane materials created heavy smoke for the first arriving Gosforth crews and four pumps and an emergency tender from Gosforth, Wallsend and Whitley Bay attended the incident.

Station Officer Bobby Bolam (immediately to the right of Rothbury's Dennis water tender) retired in 1969, having served for thirty years. (Courtesy of Angus Patterson)

Panic seems to prevail at Widdrington Social Club as the premises are gutted by fire in March 1970. Ashington's water tender crew and the station officer will have their work cut out.

The oldest appliance in the fleet had now been in service for twenty years and in view of the future need for replacement a reserve fund had been started to build up enough capital to initiate a replacement programme in 1971/72. The position now, though, was that spares for some of the older machines were no longer available and some difficulty was foreseen in keeping the vehicles serviceable until new ones could be bought. As a short term measure, the situation was alleviated somewhat by dismantling the original Whitson and Carmichael water tenders and using them as spares sources, replacing them with the two former AFS emergency pumps. The Warwickshire water tender, originally bought for the reserve fleet, was also cannibalised and never entered operational service with the brigade. There were still six former NFS Coventry Climax 500gpm trailer pumps in the brigade but these were now surplus to requirements and were offered to the council's highways department. These aging pumps were surplus to requirements after a decision made in 1970 to convert the six hose/personnel carriers into emergency tenders. During the fifteen years that the vehicles had been on the strength they had seen very little use for the purpose they were initially designed for, fortunately, and the low mileages on the appliances could not justify early disposal. During the conversion process the water tanks and hose racks were removed and in their place they were fitted out to carry breathing apparatus sets, lighting equipment and road accident extrication equipment. The opportunity was taken during the conversion to replace the outdated orange blinker lights and single bell with one blue light and a set of two-tone horns. Externally they differed little from their original form except for the lettering 'EMERGENCY TENDER' in gold above the side lockers. Following the conversion, Morpeth and Newburn were allocated two examples. The other four remained at their original locations.

The last of the trailer pumps were withdrawn in the 1970s. A Coventry Climax model is seen hitched up to the hose carrier at Alnwick. (courtesy Ian Moore)

The first emergency tender conversion was unveiled at headquarters in September 1970. It is pictured here displaying the various items of equipment carried following the conversion.

It will be recalled that some years earlier the chief fire officer had been asked to investigate alternative methods of calling in the retained men because of the distressing noise of the air-raid sirens. Well, in 1970 a suitable alternative was finally proposed when the Home Office announced details of a new radio alerting system. The equipment, available on rental through the Home Office Wireless Organisation, consisted of a pocket alerter carried by the on-call firemen, which when activated would not disturb the whole neighbourhood. There was no argument from the brigade regarding the need to introduce this equipment, but because the expected initial allocations were limited, together with the inevitable financial constraints, it was decided to introduce them over a phased period, preferably within two years. By 1972, as planned, all stations with on-call firemen had been equipped with the new system. The sirens sounded their mournful wails no more. The introduction of the new pocket alerter gave the firemen much more freedom.

Construction of a new fire station for Berwick was finally given consent and tenders were duly invited. In accordance with previous estimations, serious thought was given to the establishment of a new fire station at Cramlington. The new town had now reached a population of 15,000 and featured thirteen new factories, matching almost exactly the rate of growth predicted in 1961 when the idea of a new fire station was first mooted. It was thought that the rate of growth would continue in future years, increasing the fire risk and therefore the need for fire cover. It was agreed that a new fire station should be established in the town, the construction to commence not later than 1 April 1971. It was planned that the station would comprise of three bays to accommodate two pumping appliances and an emergency tender. Being a new town, for once there was an abundance of suitable sites. Tenders for the erection of Rothbury's new station were advertised in March, and for Newburn it was proposed that a suitable site already

In 1972 plans were finally approved for the erection of a replacement station for Berwick. The original is pictured here in 1950.

earmarked at Throckley should be purchased and construction commence as soon as Home Office approval was given. The county's Finance Committee disagreed, though, and decided that the purchase should be deferred. This did not go down too well with Newburn UDC, which had expended a considerable amount of expense on land reclamation to make the site suitable. The matter was referred back to the council for further discussion. This deferral turned out to be a very shrewd decision, given events to follow, but it would not be without some criticism.

At the end of 1970 Divisional Officer J.B. Harkins retired after completing thirty years of service. Formerly with the Edinburgh Fire Brigade, he came to Northumberland on its formation in 1948 and was the person primarily responsible for sustaining the operational efficiency of obsolete wartime appliances. In 1953 he was promoted to divisional officer in charge of the North Division, and in 1962, after further promotion, was placed in charge of the South Division. His departure marked the last of the uniformed officers appointed on the formation of the brigade.

In 1971 a government White Paper announced proposals that would radically change the make-up of Great Britain's counties and county borough councils, Northumberland being no

Divisional Officer Harkins was the last of the original 1948 officers to retire. He left the brigade in 1970.

exception. Briefly, the paper stated that 'if local authorities are to provide services effectively and economically their area should be large enough in size, population and resources to meet administrative needs, including the maintenance and development of a trained and expert local government service; boundaries should be drawn so that areas take account of patterns of development and travel; and services which are closely linked should be in the hands of the same authority'. The White Paper proposed the creation of four new counties for the Northeast. Northumberland would remain, but would lose the boroughs of Wallsend and Whitley Bay, the urban districts of Gosforth, Longbenton, Newburn and Seaton Valley, the parishes of Brunswick, Dinnington, Hazlerigg, Heddon-on-the-Wall, North Gosforth, Ponteland and Woolsington, and the Moot Hall and precincts in Newcastle. All of these areas were to become part of the new Metropolitan County of Tyne and Wear. Presumably Northumberland would still be large enough in size, population and resources to meet administrative needs and so on. If the proposals went ahead, Northumberland County Fire Brigade would lose four of its busiest fire stations. Time would tell.

CHAPTER 6

NEW APPLIANCES

Problems associated with the age of the current appliances, and the need for additional appliances at Cramlington, were becoming acute. It was accepted that the current fire appliance fleet was about to become obsolete and positive plans were now made to decide a replacement programme, taking advantage of current developments in capacity and design, to provide once again a uniform standard of appliance. Suggestions were put forward to buy Home Office specification chassis with bodies added by local builders. Pumps from existing appliances could be fitted and the hydraulic equipment and ancillaries added by brigade workshop staff. It was estimated that pumps purchased by this arrangement would cost about £4,700 as against £7,140 from a recognised fire appliance manufacturer. Considering the 'home-built' scheme, it was agreed in principle to purchase sixteen chassis between 1971 and 1975 at a total saving of £37,000. The chief fire officer and the brigade's transport manager, Herbert Mardon, drew up design specifications, and orders for the first two chassis were placed in mid-1971 with Davidson & Sons of Whitley Bay. The chassis selected was the Ford 'D' series with turbocharged diesel engines. The contract for the bodywork was awarded to George Hallowell of Morpeth. It was planned to build a further six the following year and another eight before 1975, making the total up to the required sixteen. A further nine chassis were ordered early in the following year, three for the new Cramlington station which was now under construction, and the other six for the general replacement programme. Of four tenders received for the second batch of new appliances, Messrs Pattersons & Co. of Newcastle submitted the lowest tender and consequently became the suppliers, and local firm Hallowells of Morpeth was once again awarded the contracts for the bodywork for all of the pumps and the Cramlington emergency tender.

Hexham's new fire station came a step closer when land on Tyne Mills Industrial Estate was purchased for the site of the town's new fire station. At headquarters some welcome financial remuneration came when Northumberland County Council Health Department secured arrangements to use part of the transport workshops for the maintenance and servicing of the county's ambulances. This arrangement carried on until well after the county's ambulances were transferred to the Area Health Authority in April 1974, when mergers saw the formation of the Northumbria Ambulance Service. There would be some other joint location schemes in the not too distant future.

In October Wooler was in the thick of things when fire raged through farm buildings at Wooperton, six miles outside of the town. Thousands of tons of baled hay, farm buildings and drums of chemical fertiliser were heavily involved in fire, fanned by gales, and there was considerable risk to the fire crews when the drums of highly explosive fertiliser burst open during the firefighting operations. Reinforcements were dispatched from Belford, Seahouses,

Alnwick and Morpeth and, because of the risk of contamination, the brigade's control and decontamination units from Morpeth also attended what was one of the biggest farm fires in the area for years. A nearby duck pond and stream were used as convenient water supplies. The farm steward who raised the alarm commended the firemen's quick response and praised highly the 'wonderful job' that was done.

In February 1972 a Certificate of Merit from the RSPCA was awarded to members of Alnwick Fire Brigade for the rescue of a pony from quicksand at Powburn. In July Seahouses and another Alnwick crew received a similar certificate for their rescue of three bullocks trapped in a cesspit. This was the third such award for Alnwick personnel: two years earlier the station had received a certificate for their rescue of a dog from the River Coquet.

It was the county's turn to request assistance from the Newcastle and Tynemouth brigades in 1972, when, on the early afternoon of 4 April, a large fabrication shed at Davy Bank, Wallsend, became heavily involved in fire. Both appliances from Wallsend arrived at the Yarrow Engineering premises to find a severe fire spreading rapidly along the roof. Fortunately an abundant water supply was available from the nearby River Tyne to supply the ten pumps and

This large fabrication shed at Yarrow Engineering, Wallsend, was the scene of Northumberland's biggest fire for many years.

two turntable ladders that were required to extinguish the blaze. Restricted access to the yard because of a low railway bridge necessitated crews slipping the wheeled escapes from appliances and leaving them on Hadrian Road before they could gain entry.

There were many standby moves for appliances to cover empty stations, one unusual one being Prudhoe standing in at Gosforth. In June the brigade were back at High Gosforth Park for a fire that destroyed over seven acres of standing timber. This early afternoon call, on an untypically hot summer's day, involved long hose lays and water relays from hydrants and open water in the park. Five pumps from Gosforth, Wallsend, Morpeth and Whitley Bay and an emergency tender were engaged at this fire until the afternoon of the following day. They were back in the park again in August when the John Jacobs Golf Centre caught fire. A total of five pumps were ordered to this fire, including one from Newcastle, where once again long hose lays were required to extinguish the blaze, but not before the groundsman's caravan was completely destroyed and the wooden club house severely damaged. An unusual hazard at this fire was the hundreds of yellow golf balls floating about in inches of water that caused the firemen to enact some strange balancing acts during the course of damping down operations.

On 14 June, amidst much ceremony, the first of the brigade's new Ford water tenders was revealed to members of the Fire Brigades Committee and the press. Delivered some eight years after the last Commer delivery, the new appliance was a startling contrast to the others in the fleet. Most notable was the unpainted aluminium finish for the bodywork and the large gallows that supported the appliance's 45ft light alloy extension ladder. This new addition marked the

The prototype Ford on receipt from the coachbuilders. All of the firefighting equipment was fitted by the transport workshop staff.

The prototype Northumberland Ford pictured on the day that it was unveiled to the press. Registered CTY 380K it was later re-registered as ENL 734L.

Another picture of the first of Northumberland's second generation pumping appliances. An unpainted example can be seen in the background.

beginning of the withdrawal of the traditional wheeled escapes. Additionally the appliances had a dual function and were designated as water tender ladder/emergency tenders. To adopt this designation, the abundance of locker space allowed the machines to carry a variety of light and medium rescue equipment, particularly for attending road accidents in the county. As the new appliances came on line, the Karrier emergency tenders were gradually withdrawn, marking the end of special appliances in the brigade for some years to come. The appliances were rather plain in looks and lacked the chrome embellishments of the Commers. Nevertheless they were functional and that is what counted.

In October 1972, Northumberland's fire engines were back in Sunderland assisting the County Borough Brigade at a major fire at Hardy's furniture store in the town centre. This midday fire required the attendance of twenty pumps before it was brought under control. Two appliances from Wallsend were dispatched, thanks to the Tyne Tunnel now being in operation, and a Whitley Bay appliance was sent to the town to provide fire cover at Sunderland's central fire station, being turned out on two occasions while on standby. This was the second and last occasion that a Northumberland appliance worked in Sunderland (the first was at Christmas 1957 when three of the county's pumps were dispatched to Jopling's department store).

As 1973 progressed, the brigade was still facing a busy time with serious fires. During the second week of April fire ripped through the factory of Blyth dye and fabric finishers Atkinson Throwster on the Kitty Brewster Trading Estate. The midnight blaze started in a ventilation shaft and quickly engulfed the roof before spreading throughout the entire premises. Intense efforts to prevent tanks of oil used in the fabric processing area of the plant from exploding were successful, but, despite the best efforts of the firefighters, dawn broke to reveal a twisted mass of girders. In all, ten pumps from Blyth, Whitley Bay, Morpeth, Ashington, Wallsend,

In November 1972 the Brown Memorial Hall in Amble was gutted by fire but the town's crew managed to prevent serious damage to the adjoining United Reform Church. (Courtesy of Photo Centre, Berwick)

Eighteen years passed between Northumberland's two incursions into the Borough of Sunderland. On the second occasion, Wallsend's water tender is pictured after arriving at Hardy's furniture store fire in October 1972. (Courtesy of Newcastle Chronicle & Journal)

Gosforth and Cramlington were called to the blaze, and units from Newcastle & Gateshead Joint Fire Service were moved into the southern areas of the county to provide cover at the depleted stations.

In August the county was faced with another major fire at Wallsend, when fire destroyed the roof of a large two-storey building belonging to Graham Moats Ltd, at Davy Bank, not far from Yarrow Engineering. Eight main jets from ten pumps and a turntable ladder were needed to extinguish the fire. Appliances from Tynemouth and Newcastle & Gateshead Brigades assisted the county and, for the first time in the brigade's history, the reinforcements included two appliances from Durham County Fire Brigade, making the short journey through the Tyne Tunnel from Hebburn.

The mutual aid obligations between Northumberland County and Newcastle & Gateshead Fire Authorities were terminated on 1 April 1974 following local government reorganisation. This picture depicts a joint turnout arrangement at the notorious Dorrington Road area of Fawdon.

The initial construction programme of the new Ford water tenders became a considerable cause for concern in 1973. By the end of March, six out of the nine that should have been completed had still not been started. The appointed coachbuilders had failed to meet the delivery dates and agreed to an unconditional termination of the contract. Two of the chassis that required bodies were transferred to Killingworth Coachworks, which promised completion by March 1974. This firm also found it difficult to adhere to the completion schedules, so not without some difficulty another firm had to be found to continue with the construction. North-East Vehicle Builders Ltd of Prudhoe was thus awarded the contract for bodies to be built on the remaining four chassis of the original orders. This latter firm continued with the building programme and bodied the remainder of the locally built Ford water tenders. The initial delays with production and delivery resulted in the original financial estimates increasing somewhat, but they still worked out cheaper than appliances constructed by the major fire appliance engineers. The delivery of these new appliances marked the gradual death knell of the wheeled escape ladders in the county, but not in the country as a whole, as the London Fire Brigade, still big operators of this type of equipment, bought four surplus examples from Northumberland.

A site for a new Blyth fire station needed to be identified this year and was to be the last of the brigade's stations to be replaced under the original station replacement programme, excepting the four stations that were being transferred to Tyne and Wear. Amble still needed replacing but a site had already been found for this. Cramlington fire station was completed well ahead of its original estimate and ready for occupation and a site was secured for Amble's new station.

Newburn's classically styled prewar fire station did not meet with the approval of the new Tyne & Wear Metropolitan Fire Authority, which inherited the building in April 1974.

Whitley Bay fire station in 1971. To the right of the picture was a garage that housed the emergency tender and AFS appliances. Transferred to Tyne & Wear in 1974, the station was later disbanded in favour of fire cover from Tynemouth.

CHAPTER 7

THE REORGANISATION OF 1974

During the previous twenty-six years the brigade had undergone vast changes in every aspect, from personnel and appliances to premises and workload, to the credit of all members of the brigade. However, nothing would match the changes that occurred on 1 April 1974. Following the 1971 announcement of the Local Government Reorganisation Act regarding boundary changes, the proposed formation of new counties did take place throughout the country and in April many counties amalgamated and new counties were formed. Some counties disappeared and all former county boroughs became incorporated into these new authorities. Britain's fire brigades were reduced in number from 152 down to fifty-two. Northumberland County was not excluded from the scheme and, as proposed, it lost four fire stations to the newly formed Tyne and Wear Metropolitan Fire Brigade, which encompassed areas north of the River Tyne down to the southern area of the River Wear. Under this reorganisation the separate fire brigades of Newcastle & Gateshead, Tynemouth, Sunderland and South Shields ceased to exist as such. In addition, Northumberland was compelled to transfer its four busiest stations, Gosforth, Newburn, Whitley Bay and Wallsend, to the new authority, together with the personnel and eight appliances that were housed at these premises. During the years of attachment to Northumberland, serious plans had been made to acquire a site to replace Newburn fire station, and sites had been secured for Gosforth and Wallsend, but a site for Whitley Bay's replacement had never been considered because of a more urgent need to replace the former temporary NFS stations. Just before the appointed day, an exchange of appliances took place when the brigade's four newest machines were transferred from Berwick, Morpeth and Ashington to Gosforth and Wallsend. This generous move had various motives behind it, but did not appease the new Tyne and Wear Brigade. As early as January it was reported in the press that firemen would refuse to use ten fire-fighting appliances transferred from Northumberland County to the Tyne and Wear Metropolitan Fire Brigade on 1 April because of their antiquated state. The Fire Brigades' Union in Newcastle advised its members not to turn out in 'museum pieces' which were so old that 'the men were handicapped when using them'. There was also criticism directed towards the fire stations, which were said to have been in a 'deplorable condition'. Newburn was described as being 'shocking, unsanitary and rat-infested'. The dissatisfaction continued into November when a press article described the former Northumberland appliances as being 'obstacles and in bad condition'. This legacy of inherited appliances 'left much to be desired'. In reply to these allegations, Chief Fire Officer Henshaw described the actions of the union as 'irresponsible' and stated that the fact that a machine was twenty years old did not mean that it was not functional. During their time in Northumberland the machines had never failed. This was quite true. They had been good, solid, reliable appliances, ideally suited for the varied risks in the county, and it had already been recognised that replacement was indeed due but this couldn't be rectified overnight. Pat Watters, the chief fire officer of the new Metropolitan Brigade, expressed his disappointment at the quality of some of the appliances that were being transferred from one of the county areas and said that in his opinion 'they should not be on the road'. Appliances were not the only item of concern publicised by the forthcoming Metropolitan Fire Brigade. Criticism was also levelled at the manning arrangements at the Northumberland stations. Northumberland 'as it exists at present is severely undermanned', said Chief Officer Watters. He stated that the brigade only managed to operate on a system of overtime whereby men in some stations were working a 56-hour week, together with undertaking retained duties, amounting in some cases to being on call for 120 hours a week. In reality these duties were undertaken at the request of the firemen concerned and approaches had already been made to Tyne and Wear for these arrangements to continue after the merger. The union spokesman, however, was quite adamant: 'We will not allow this. No man in this brigade will do retained shifts for the county.'

The Northumberland County Fire Brigade was a much smaller authority now. Four full-time and retained fire stations had been lost, but one new one was operational at Cramlington. The last committee meeting of Northumberland County Fire Brigade in its original form was held on 21 January 1974 and was over in a record 20 minutes. At the meeting Alderman Mrs Janie Heppell thanked the chairman, Councillor John Collingwood, for his work over the past years, and also praised the work of Chief Fire Officer Henshaw.

Recapping on the achievements and developments that had taken place during the previous twenty-six years, it will be recalled that the 1948 establishment comprised nine full-time and ten part-time fire stations manned by 181 full-time firemen and 244 part-time firemen. There were nine firewomen attached to the brigade control and fourteen administrative staff. The combination of progress, together with the effects of reduced hours of duty for firemen, provided the 1974 establishment of eleven full-time stations and ten part-time stations, with 288 full-time and 240 part-time firemen, thirteen firewomen and eighteen administrative staff. From 1 April the number of full-time stations was reduced to seven. Part-time stations remained unaltered and personnel numbered 199 full-time and 170 part-time firemen, with no change in the numbers of firewomen and administrative staff. As well as the completion of a new headquarters, additional fire stations had been established at Ashington and Cramlington, and replacement full-time stations built at Alnwick, Morpeth, Berwick and Hexham. Nine out of ten part-time stations had been replaced, leaving only two of the brigade's stations left to replace: one part-time station, Amble, and one whole-time station, Blyth. During the period in question the services of the brigade had been called upon on 59,000 occasions and over the years the incidence of calls had shown a remarkably consistent increase from 1,200 in 1948 to 4,400 in 1973. It would be interesting to see what developments took place in Northumberland during the following twenty-eight years.

CHAPTER 8

THE NEW BRIGADE

From 1974 onwards Northumberland County Fire Brigade was a much smaller organisation. The four busiest fire stations in the most urbanised parts of the county had now left the jurisdiction of the county council. The mutual aid scheme with neighbouring brigades was amended somewhat, with Tyne and Wear now being the one where most aid would be given and received. In the early days of the new authorities Northumberland was often prompted to request assistance from Tyne and Wear, particularly in the Cramlington, Weetslade and Castle Ward areas, and this once again invited some criticism from Tyne and Wear's FBU representative. It was claimed that public safety was being put at risk because Tyne and Wear appliances were travelling out of the area, leaving gaps in fire cover in Tyne and Wear. During the previous twelve months there had been 200 attendances in Northumberland, as opposed to about forty in the other direction. Maybe someone had forgotten, but in the last year of Northumberland's original configuration the brigade had provided assistance to neighbouring brigades, predominantly Newcastle & Gateshead, on 483 occasions.

Gosforth and Newburn were still providing free fire cover to Ponteland, which remained within Northumberland, based on assurances that a new fire station would be in place by 1977. Efforts had been made to resolve the situation of cover at Ponteland, as provision was being made to establish a retained station in the town, hopefully with construction commencing in 1976 and a completion date of early 1977. As a stopgap, plans were pursued to institute temporary fire cover from Newcastle Airport. The Civil Airport Committee agreed in principle to provide accommodation for an appliance at the airport, manned in part by airport firemen who lived sufficiently nearby, and with an assumption that they would be prepared to undertake such responsibility. This arrangement, if successful, would have enabled the brigade to provide adequate fire cover to Ponteland without any significant capital expenditure and it was planned to start on 1 April. Alas, nothing came of these novel and ambitious plans and the problems of fire cover at Ponteland remained an increasingly urgent matter for the foreseeable future.

On a more positive note, Berwick's new fire station in Ord Road, Tweedmouth, went operational on 22 August 1974 and the old premises at Wallace Green were sold back to the council. Four months later, the long-standing problems at Hexham finally came to an end with the opening of a new three-bay station at Abbey Mills on 10 December. Amble was next for replacement and a site was secured the same year for that development.

A major change to national fire brigade organisation occurred when the firemen's working week was reduced from 56 hours to 48 hours. This reduction resulted in an additional fourth watch having to be introduced. As well as the traditional red, white and blue watches, there was now a green watch. Firemen's shifts now consisted of two days, two nights and four off, after which the cycle repeated itself. This additional watch resulted in a massive recruitment operation to fill the vacancies; the new system went live on 8 November.

Not long after the formation of the restyled brigade, Hexham crews received much public acclaim in May, following the difficult rescue of a badly injured workman trapped by heavy masonry and suspended upside down from the top of 35ft of steel scaffolding at Battle Hill, Hexham. The crew received a commendation and mention in orders for a job 'expertly done under difficult and potentially dangerous circumstances'. Almost one year earlier, a letter of appreciation had been received from the manager of the historic White Swan Hotel in Alnwick in respect of a fire that severely damaged the historic hostelry on 11 May. This fire was attended by crews from Alnwick, Amble, Seahouses and Rothbury. According to the chief fire officer, the nature and occupancy of the property resulted in a battle that was fraught with potential for disaster. The fact that the fire was contained without loss of life or even serious injury reflected great credit upon all concerned.

The first big fire for the new brigade occurred in the early morning of 22 June 1975, when the seventy-year-old Seaton Deleval Social Club was engulfed in fire. Flames were already through the roof when the Blyth crews arrived and damage to the extent of £200,000 was the ultimate result. Sixty firemen attended the blaze, including some from neighbouring Tyne and Wear.

In May 1976 the rescue of a trapped driver from an overturned Land Rover by the River Coquet ford at Warkworth earned Sub Officer Douglas Leek and Firemen Ronald Wintrip and David Doleman commendations from the chairman of the council and the Fire Brigades Committee for undertaking the rescue in extremely hazardous conditions.

At the August meeting of the Fire Brigades Committee it was announced, much to the surprise of the members, that Chief Fire Officer Henshaw was intending to retire at the end of the year. He had been awarded the Queen's Fire Service Medal during the year. His short tenure as chief officer, when compared to that of his predecessor, saw amongst other things the development of a comprehensive communication system and the continual fulfilment of the building programme for new and replacement stations. He was leaving to undertake a two-year tour of duty as inspector of fire services to the government of Zambia. Deputy Chief Fire Officer Colin Bates filled the vacancy.

The summer of 1976 was the longest and hottest on record for Britain for many years and the shortfall of rain naturally resulted in a big increase in the number of grass and heath fires in the county. In the twenty-four weeks from the start of April there was a 57 per cent increase in calls compared to the same period in 1975. Altogether, by the end of the year the brigade had tackled 1,735 fires on top of the usual false alarms and special service calls.

After many tribulations Ponteland got its new fire station, which was officially opened in April 1977, although it did not go operational until 11 May. Originally supplied with one of the Dennis/Miles water tenders, some embarrassment resulted when the station was later assigned a Ford water tender, which was found to be too high for the appliance room. The matter was resolved by lowering the floor sufficiently to provide greater headroom.

The end of the year saw a situation that was never before thought possible in the history of the British fire services: a national strike in support of a wage rise. In November the nation's firemen withdrew their labour after talks with the government's negotiators broke down. Most of the firefighting resources in Northumberland ceased to operate, although the rural retained fire stations continued to meet their obligations, but only in their individual station areas. The remainder of the county was covered by armed forces personnel manning former Home Office/AFS Green Goddess engines from Territorial Army premises, police stations or hospitals. Each one was accompanied by a police car acting as escort and communications vehicle. Of course

Colin Bates was Northumberland's third chief fire officer.

The old Blyth Dry Dock and Shipbuilding Company later ignominiously became used for ship breaking. In August 1976, waste oil caused a fire requiring the attendance of four appliances. (Courtesy of Newcastle Chronicle & Journal*)*

Appliances from Berwick, Belford and Alnwick attended a dust explosion that destroyed some of the grain bins at Tweed Valley Maltings in December 1976.

the rapidly trained and inexperienced manpower was no match for the professional expertise of the local authority fire service, but in the circumstances this was what was available. In addition to the Green Goddesses, a limited number of specialised breathing apparatus teams and foam tender appliances of RAF descent were distributed throughout the country. The strike carried on throughout the Christmas and New Year period and was to last for a total of nine weeks before the workforce settled for a wage deal that linked annual increases to the upper quartile of male manual workers. This deal was supposed to ensure that the fire service would never be placed in a similar position again. Unfortunately this was not the case. Nationally, the situation was now resolved but locally there was more strife in the offing.

During 1978 serious consideration was being given to amendments to the manning of the county's fire engines. Of the thirty-nine shire counties in the country Northumberland was among three with the lowest average of fires per head of population. Despite this, and alarmingly for the Audit Commission that was looking into the finances of Northumberland County Council, the brigade had the highest relative expenses of any county fire authority. The Audit Commission recommended the axing of 24-hour cover at five of Northumberland's fire stations. The situation was looked at in some depth, especially in connection with the fire stations at Alnwick, Berwick and Hexham, which had been called out just 132, 157 and 205 times respectively between November 1976 and October 1977. Serious consideration was given to downgrading these stations from full-time manning to day manning, which would result in the loss of forty-two full-time posts and proposed savings of £1 million. Many heated discussions took place between the Home Office, the county council and the FBU, and in February 1979 it was accepted in principle that day manning was the way forward. However, the matter was deferred for two years. It would not stay at rest for long, though. The people of Northumberland were privileged, apparently, to have the Rolls Royce of fire brigades.

Three Cramlington firemen were taken to hospital on 8 March 1979 after one of the Ford water tenders overturned on the way to a fire. The three-year-old engine overturned on a sharp left-hand bend just after the driver had taken the Annitsford turning off the Spine Road roundabout while en-route to a grass fire at Annitsford. All four crewmembers managed to free themselves without assistance and fortunately the injuries sustained were minor. None of the crew was detained in hospital although the fire engine was extensively damaged and needed a complete rebuild. The accident was put down to the machine skidding on a patch of diesel oil.

Northumberland was still committed to replacing its aging fleet of 1950s Commer and Dennis fire engines, and as 1979 drew to a close Muir's appliance replacement programme was virtually complete, with a total of eighteen of the locally built Ford appliances in service. The emergency tender, originally ordered for Cramlington fire station, had been conspicuous by its absence and eventually appeared in 1980 equipped as a decontamination unit for deployment at chemical incidents. The last of the original Commer water tenders was finally withdrawn, with the last three being sold in late 1980. Strangely enough, one of these was the oldest appliance in the fleet

Two of these Angloco-bodied Ford water tenders were delivered in 1980 to supplement the locally built appliances. This one was stationed at Alnwick.

Amble and Seahouses brigades attended this bungalow fire at Bamburgh in July 1980. The Amble appliance illustrated still looks good despite its twenty-four years of service. (Courtesy of Newcastle Chronicle & Journal*)*

– the first of the Miles Commers, which was delivered in 1951 and by the time of disposal had served for just under thirty years. By the time the programme ended there was still a shortfall of five appliances and additional vehicles, still on Ford chassis, were ordered from established fire engine coachbuilders. During the year a smart new water tender ladder with coachwork by HCB-Angus of Totton, Southampton, was delivered and placed in service at Cramlington. Four more with bodywork by Yorkshire-based Angloco were ordered, two for delivery in 1981 and the second two the year after. The appliance fleet was once again very much standardised, this time on Ford chassis. All of the Karrier emergency tenders had been sold off and the disposal of the remaining former retained Rolls Dennis machines was imminent.

The remote areas of the county continued to pose threats. At 8 p.m. on 4 April 1980, fifty firemen were involved in fighting a moorland and plantation fire that stretched over a one-mile front at Harbottle Crag plantation near Rothbury. Just as Muir had feared forty years earlier, the fire was raging out of control as high winds fanned the flames. Because of the rough terrain firemen couldn't get their vehicles close enough to the fire and as water supplies were almost none existent, beaters had to be used to try to extinguish the fire. Three hours into the blaze the flames entered the Kidland Forest, threatening to destroy £500,000-worth of young trees. Forestry Commission staff were mobilised to assist the firefighters and, like a sign from the gods, the wind suddenly dropped and changed direction, giving the fire brigade the welcome respite that was needed. By the time the fire was brought under control, it had stretched two miles. This incident, which saw the destruction of fifty acres of moorland and 40,000 trees, was declared the county's biggest plantation fire since the war. A spate of dry weather coupled with very high winds had resulted in tinder dry conditions, making the situation critical for this type of fire. Ten days later, 30 acres of young trees on the slopes of the Cheviot Hills were destroyed by fire and required the combined efforts of crews from Wooler, Belford and Alnwick, together with the assistance of estate workers, to extinguish. During the same period, fire ravaged two square miles of moorland and two plantations of trees at Emblehope Farm near Bellingham.

In August, Seaton Valley Co-operative Society's building on Fontburn Road became heavily involved in fire in a midnight blaze. Forty firemen with six pumps from Blyth, Cramlington, Morpeth and Ashington attended the blaze, during which thirteen families in the vicinity of the fire had to be evacuated. On arrival the upper floors and storage bays were heavily smoke-logged and twelve men wearing breathing apparatus were detailed to enter the building to try to find the seat of the fire.

Colin Bates served as chief fire officer for only a short time; in April 1981 he retired and was replaced by Bob Wilson, his deputy. His tenure was equally short-lived and his successor was an outsider, the former deputy chief officer of Cleveland Fire Brigade, Dennis Mee. Both of these chief fire officers had the major problem of addressing the recommendations of the Audit Commission's report, and various options were proposed. The situation was not aided by a further reduction in the firemen's working week from 48 hours to 42. Discussions included disbanding the retained appliances at Cramlington, Ashington, Hexham and Morpeth, and in fact all but Hexham lost their second pumps. The question of day manning was still foremost as a means of reducing expenditure. Chief Fire Officer Wilson had put forward a scheme for

The aftermath of the Seaton Valley Co-operative Society fire. Cramlington and Blyth crews prepare to make up equipment.

phased manpower reduction as an alternative to day manning, but the introduction of the 42-hour week a year later meant that the number of full-time firemen increased to 256 and the retained crew at Morpeth was reintroduced.

On top of this it was suggested that fire cover in the Kielder region needed improving, and it was proposed that a new fire station be established at Kielder, which was usually covered by the retained station at Bellingham. It was also suggested that there was a need for a turntable ladder fire appliance in the county, as many buildings were over 40ft high. At an estimated cost of £80,000, this project was not proceeded with despite a demonstration being arranged with the UK agent Angloco and the French ladder manufacturer, Riffaud. However, four more water tenders were ordered this year, heralding another major change in type. These appliances were based on the Dodge G1313, oddly enough descendants of the original Commer appliances, but with bodywork by Carmichael and Sons of Worcester, a company that supplied Northumberland's second postwar appliance. The four were assigned to Ashington, Blyth, Cramlington and Morpeth. The deliveries of these saw the disposal of the last vestiges of the once proud Miles fleet, when the last three Rolls-Royce-powered Dennis water tenders went through the auctions at Birtley, Tyne and Wear. They had given twenty-five years of service. The oldest appliance in the fleet was now ten years old, and there were no more new pump deliveries for seven years.

CHAPTER 9

FIRE AND RESCUE

In September 1982 it was announced that the original Northumberland County Fire Brigade title was to be replaced by a new designation that reflected the changing workload of the modern fire brigade. Henceforth, the Northumberland County Fire Brigade was to be known as Northumberland Fire & Rescue Service.

The first of four Dodge Commando water tender ladders on the forecourt at Morpeth with the retained locally built Ford water tender. Both appliances later underwent complete refurbishments.

Problems became evident with the existing water tender fleet around this time, when it was identified that most of the locally built Ford water tenders, introduced in 1972, were beginning to show signs of severe wood rot in the framework. As a result, all of them had to undergo a total rebuild of the rear bodywork. One by one the appliances were stripped down in the workshops and rebuilt with new framework and aluminium panels, and when completed they had a slightly different appearance. The first one to be rebuilt, a 1973 model, was assigned to Bellingham, having previously been used as a driver training vehicle. The next three were relocated to Haltwhistle, Rothbury and Allendale. These conversions kept the workshops busy for some years.

On Sunday 18 October 1983 Allendale was called out to a fire that eventually required four pumps before it was brought under control. Just after noon the brigade turned out to the Ashleigh Hotel in the town, where it was obvious that the fire was serious. A second appliance was requested while the first was still en route to the fire. Hexham's water tender was immediately dispatched and on arrival it was found that a second floor bathroom and bedroom were severely enveloped in flame. There was a possibility that someone was still inside the building, although it was ascertained that eight people had previously been evacuated. Having gained entry into the building, the crew was able to rescue a woman from the premises. A further two appliances, from Hexham and Haydon Bridge, were dispatched to the building, which was now heavily smoke-logged, with flames licking from the roof. With the use of two main jets and two hose reels, the fire was eventually brought under control.

Eight days later, ten pumps raced to Haltwhistle, when the westernmost station in the county was once again faced with a major fire on its home ground. One of the longest hose relays to be

Fifty sick people had to be hastily evacuated when fire gutted two bedrooms at Dilston Hall in September 1982. Four pumps attended the blaze. (Courtesy of Newcastle Chronicle & Journal*)*

It was a miracle that there was no loss of life or serious injuries at the second Morpeth train crash. (Courtesy of Newcastle Chronicle & Journal)

set up in the county was established to help save the remote Dunholme Farm at the top of Comb Hill, Haltwhistle. The flames from 3,000 bales of burning straw and hay could be seen by the Haltwhistle crew as they turned out from the station, leaving them in no doubt as to what was facing them. The farmer and his son evacuated a dozen head of cattle from a byre before flames from the adjacent hay barn engulfed the structure. Appliances also attended from Cumberland and Durham in what was, according to a brigade spokesman 'one of the biggest combined operations' ever tackled. Owing to the narrow roads near the farm, many water tenders were tied up ferrying water in a circuitous route via the town of Haltwhistle. This incident, and the earlier one at Smith and Walton's paint works (at which some of the retained firemen were employed in their regular occupations), were the only ten-pump fires that Haltwhistle ever had to attend. Fires of this magnitude were, and still are, rare in the rural parts of the county.

On 24 June 1983 the east coast main railway line from London to Edinburgh was the scene of another major incident when, fifteen years after the earlier Morpeth train derailment, another similar incident occurred in the same location. Just after thirty minutes past midnight, the overnight Aberdeen to Kings Cross sleeper train, consisting of seven sleeping cars and two brake coaches, was derailed on the notorious Morpeth curve, jack-knifing and overturning coaches, two of which ended up embedded in the sides of adjacent bungalows. When the fire brigade arrived, the crews were met with the sight of people on tops of coaches assisting with the escape of other passengers. Thorough searches of the carriages were undertaken by the rescue workers and it was fortunate that on this occasion there were no fatalities. Of the seventy-seven passengers and staff involved in the incident, thirty-seven needed hospital treatment, of whom only three were detained. By 4 a.m. the incident was deemed to be under control. The absence of fatalities at this second incident was partly attributable to the stronger construction of modern railway carriages. Seven appliances attended this incident.

In 1985 Chief Fire Officer Dennis Mee announced his retirement. The deputy chief fire officer at this time was John Weddle, who had spent his entire career in Northumberland. As he declined to seek promotion, the post of chief fire officer was awarded to a young officer from Kent Fire Brigade by the name of Jeff Ord. A native of Sunderland, Mr Ord had followed in the footsteps of his father and uncle, beginning his fire brigade career with the Sunderland Fire Brigade. Various moves between brigades saw his career move forward in this appointment in Northumberland, although there would be other moves in the future.

Among many other things, probably the greatest achievement of Mee's tenure was the establishment of a fire station on Holy Island. The island's residents had often worried about the consequences of a serious fire while the island was inaccessible from the mainland during

Former Sunderland fireman Jeff Ord became chief fire officer of Northumberland in 1985.

high tides. During the war, there had been a volunteer fire party on the island equipped with a hand-operated pump. Now the citizens were requesting the re-establishment of a firefighting party and consequently a garage was constructed on the island to house one of the Ford water tenders. A number of residents were given basic training to allow them to operate the appliance, pending the arrival of other resources from the mainland. Within the fire team were three female volunteers, sufficiently unusual to attract the attention of the local press. From around this time, it became more common for female firefighters to participate in active duties, particularly at the part-time stations but also at full-time establishments. This prompted the change of title from 'fireman' to the non-sexist 'firefighter'.

The islanders were certainly happy now that they had their own fire brigade and the county council was no doubt happy that some of its responsibility had been placed in the hands of the islanders themselves and, equally important, at a minimal cost. In March 1985, amid much ceremony, the Lindisfarne unit of Northumberland Fire & Rescue Service was formally established. However, things did not go as smoothly as had been hoped. Concern was expressed about the capabilities of the personnel that would man the appliance, some of them being over fifty-five years of age, beyond the normal retirement age for operational firefighters. In addition, the training was not to the minimum statutory standards for retained firemen. Amid claims of problems with insurance, it was decided to disband the organisation. There was a total of thirteen volunteers under the leadership of sixty-year-old Doug Cromarty. The controversy raged on for five years; it was revealed that there had been only five fires on the island since the brigade was established, three of them being grass fires, one a chimney and the other an overheated chip pan. A brave fight was put up by the 180 islanders, who took their case all the way to Whitehall. The county council was accused of maladministration over the proposed axing of the fire brigade and the failure to seek Home Office approval on the matter. In mitigation, the council cited the islanders' difficulties in attending training sessions because of the tides and their work commitments. Eventually, the council suggested a more practical answer was to leave a fire appliance on the island so that in the event of a fire during high tide, crews could be transported by police or RAF helicopter from Newcastle Airport or RAF Boulmer. The islanders eventually lost their valiant battle and in March 1991 the Holy Island Volunteer Fire Brigade was disbanded.

There still remained the unresolved problems of fire cover and day manning, and under Ord's leadership a full review of the fire cover and risks in the county was undertaken. The previously deferred proposals for day manning at Hexham, Alnwick and Berwick were once again brought to the fore.

Just after midnight on 29 July 1987, Haltwhistle was turned out yet again to a severe fire, this one being at Bonnyrigg Hall near Once Brewed on the Military Road. A large glow in the distance signified that a major fire was in progress, and as the appliance neared the hall it was found that the fire had broken through the roof of the unoccupied three-storey building. Reinforcements were promptly ordered so that a water relay could be set in operation from Greenlee Lough, a natural lake over a quarter of a mile away. Appliances from Hexham, Allendale, Haydon Bridge and Cumberland assisted the initial Haltwhistle crew. With the aid of three main jets and two hose reels, the fire was brought under control but not before the hall sustained severe damage.

The National Coal Board's Mines Rescue Station, which had originally provided fire cover to the area on behalf of the county council, finally closed its doors in 1987 as a result of the closure of most of the deep mines in the county. The remaining mines were reliant on the station at Houghton le Spring in County Durham.

Blyth finally got its new fire station in 1987. Councillor Mrs E. Atkinson, chairwoman of the Public Protection Committee, presided over the official opening of the three-bay station

Flames were leaping through the roof when Haltwhistle's crew arrived at the nineteenth-century Bonnyrigg Hall. Dawn broke to reveal the burned-out remains despite a heroic battle by several reinforcing crews. (Courtesy of Newcastle Chronicle & Journal)

Blyth's new fire station on Cowpen Road was officially opened in April 1985. The original establishment was set at two pumps plus the chemical incident unit. All were full-time manned. (Courtesy of Trevor Welham)

at Cowpen Road on 28 April. The new premises replaced the original fire station, which had operated from Union Street since 1924. The opening of this station meant that the brigade's postwar fire station replacement programme was virtually complete, with only Amble now needing replacement. The new station accommodated three full-time manned appliances, two pumps and an incident support unit staffed by a total of fifty-three firefighters and officers.

The major review of the existing structure and future county needs continued into 1988. As well as fire cover and risk categories, another area to be examined was the appliance fleet. By this time the fleet was already facing obsolescence and for replacements it was decided to buy custom-built rescue/water tenders instead of standard models suitably converted. For the first time in the brigade's history, a chassis of foreign manufacture was selected; two Volvo appliances with coachwork by Yorkshire-based Angloco Ltd were duly ordered for delivery during the following year. The appliance fleet was to be standardised once again, this time using Volvo appliances.

The review of standards of fire cover was completed in 1989 and resulted in the recommendation that Alnwick, Berwick and Hexham should be downgraded from 24-hour manning to daytime and retained staffing. This would see the county's establishment reduced to 203 full-time and 155 retained firefighters. This sparked much discussion, which would rumble on for years to come.

In February 1988 it was Prudhoe's turn for action. The brigade was called out to a fire at Uni-Glory's premises at Princess Way in the town. These premises, part of the Kimberly Clark group, were used for the manufacture of paper tissues. On arrival, the crew of the Prudhoe part-time appliance was met with an open compound containing over 1,000 tons of paper that was well alight. In a short space of time six pumps were ordered to the incident, including two from Tyne and Wear Fire Brigade, from which eight jets of water were brought to bear on the fire. Factory personnel, with the aid of mechanical loaders, assisted the brigade in dispersing the smouldering debris in order to extinguish hot spots.

The first of the new Volvo appliances arrived in February 1988 and was placed in service in March at Ashington. The second followed one month later and was assigned to Morpeth. These were the only two Angloco bodied machines of this particular styling to see service in Northumberland. They were readily identified by the large specially designed moulded roofs; apart from Northumberland, the only brigade operating this design of Volvo was Dyfed in Wales. Many more Volvos followed, but from a different coachbuilder. Eventually, the entire fleet would be based on Volvo chassis. Subsequent rescue water tenders were supplied with coachwork by Carmichael & Sons Ltd of Worcester and Fulton & Wylie of Falkirk in Scotland. It was planned to acquire two new appliances every year until the fleet replacement programme was fulfilled. The Volvo machines were based on the FL614 chassis, with a 4m wheelbase and a 6-litre engine developing 210bhp. They also featured automatic transmission. The fire engineering consisted of a 1,365-litre water tank and a 2,750l/min Godiva dual pressure pump and twin hose reels. The all-steel safety crew cab could comfortably accommodate six firefighters and had provision for the stowage of four Draeger breathing apparatus sets. The life expectancy of these appliances was twelve to fourteen years.

As well as these Volvos, an order was placed for a new vehicle to replace the Ford chemical incident unit at Blyth. The following year the appliance, mounted on an Iveco Turbo-Zeta chassis, was placed into service at Blyth. It was finished in an unorthodox white livery with grey roof and skirt and had an assortment of blue trimmed yellow stripes and yellow and black chequered and striped bands. Lettered up as 'Incident Support Unit', the appliance unusually had its radio call sign displayed on the outside as well as a telephone handset symbol and the emergency telephone number 999 in red on the cab doors. The white livery saved £500 on

Northumberland's first Volvo fire engine is officially handed over to the chief fire officer by the managing director of Angloco's West Yorkshire factory.

This unusual incident support unit was delivered in 1989 at a cost of £18,500. The basic white colour scheme was enhanced by the alternate yellow and black markings.

the purchase price. The appliance, fitted out primarily for dealing with chemical and radiation incidents and general pollution leaks, carried extensive gas and radiation monitoring equipment, gas-tight and splash-resistant suits, major decontamination equipment and large quantities of absorbent materials for soaking up chemical and oil spills. In the rear of the vehicle there was a control area fitted with radio equipment, mobile phone and fax machine, useful adjuncts for consulting with chemical and radiation experts. Its service was relatively short lived, for in 1994 it became a workshop van and it was disposed of in 2002.

This was one of a number of interesting special appliances acquired at around this time. A Volvo cab and chassis multi-lift unit with hydraulic hoist for transporting demountable pods was delivered in 1991 and came complete with three different modular pods. These were a command/control unit module, a breathing apparatus training chamber and a drop-side lorry platform. The philosophy behind this type of system was to reduce manpower and vehicle maintenance by requiring only one motorised vehicle to transport several pods. Regarding the individual pods, the breathing apparatus unit was designed to be taken to outlying stations in the county to perform statutory training. Working on the matchbox principle, the box-like unit was able to expand to twice its normal size when in use. Inside was a maze of crawl ways, which could be altered to produce hundreds of different permutations. Heat was provided from an in-built heater, which doubled as a smoke generator. The flat-bed module transformed the prime mover into a lorry but with the addition of a winching system, which allowed it to be used as a recovery vehicle. The control unit incorporated an area containing radios, mobile phones, video facilities, fax machine, hand-held radios and general logistics handling equipment. This equipment was contained in two-thirds of the module. The remaining third housed the command area for firefighters to discuss strategies with other services and specialist advisers. The entire system was finished in white once again. It seemed that this colour was being universally

The Volvo prime mover with control unit module pod. This unit was also painted white with yellow striping. (Courtesy of Trevor Welham)

adopted for the special appliances and other ancillary units. These included an operational support unit (stores van) mounted on a Mercedes 310D chassis.

Moorland fires continued to stretch the resources of the brigade. In July 1952 the Ridsale Forest area of Bellingham was under siege when a 4-square-mile fire raged out of control despite the efforts of fire crews from Bellingham, Haydon Bridge, Hexham, Rothbury, Ponteland, Morpeth and Alnwick. The fire started in the Wanney Craggs area and was so severe that neighbouring roads had to be closed and farms evacuated. Although the surface fires could be extinguished, the fire was also burning underground, and earth-moving equipment had to be brought in to expose these hot spots. For the first time in the history of the brigade, a helicopter was brought in to carry out an aerial bombardment of the affected moorland. Water shortages hampered the operations, and at one time it was suggested that the only way the fire could be quickly extinguished was with the aid of a couple of days of torrential rain. Three days passed before the fire was eventually brought under control.

Christmas Day was not a cause for celebration for the residents of Trinity Court, Corbridge, because just after midnight the residents were woken up by the fire alarm. Both of Hexham's appliances were immediately dispatched to the premises, where reports of someone being trapped were relayed to the first arriving crew. Four upper-storey flats were ablaze. Within thirty minutes the fire was brought under control, with the aid of an additional two pumps. Eight firemen wearing breathing apparatus and two main jets and two hose reels were needed to extinguish this fire.

Despite modern technology, one of the most appropriate ways of tackling grass and heath fires in Northumberland is still the old fashioned manual beating method.

In July 1990 the former UBU factory on Blyth Industrial Estate was severely damaged by fire. Now operated by the firm of Audis Noble, firemen were hard pressed to prevent the fire from spreading to exposed fuel tanks at the rear of the large warehouse. Five pumps attended this fire and five main jets were quickly brought to bear on the fire, restricting damage to one end of the building. This year saw Northumberland attend a record number of calls, averaging twelve each day. The total number of emergency calls was 4,579, an increase of 20 per cent over the previous year. Special service calls were up by 26 per cent and forty-three people lost their lives in fires or accidents.

A new aid to firefighting was delivered to the brigade in 1990, reminiscent of the old Bren gun carrier at Kielder. This was a four-wheeled Kawasaki Bayou quad unit and trailer acquired from Logic Trailers at Hexham, for assisting the brigade with transporting equipment and personnel to the remote areas of forest and moorland that abounded in the north and west of the county. Able to carry up to six firefighters, the four-wheel-drive unit featured a specially designed axle on the trailer unit which ensured that no matter how rough the terrain, the trailer always remained almost horizontal at all times. Also the first Land Rover vehicles (short wheelbase versions) were purchased for use in moorland; one of them was assigned to towing the Kawasaki on its custom-built trailer. They could carry up to seven firefighters and heavy payloads of firefighting and rescue equipment, therefore having the multi-functional role of personnel carrier and general purpose van. Previously Land Rovers belonging to the Forestry Commission had been used to transport personnel and equipment to remote areas.

The novel Kawasaki Bayou all-terrain vehicle cost £5,000 and had a life expectancy of twenty years.

Fires continued to be dealt with as usual and at the beginning of 1991 the popular Blackbird Inn at Ponteland was the scene of a serious teatime fire, which saw the roof and first floor suffer serious damage. Ironically, at the time of the call the Ponteland appliance was investigating a bomb hoax at the airport. Towards the end of 1992, on 12 December, Northumberland had its biggest ever fire in terms of the number of appliances needed, when the Dynoplast factory on the North Seaton industrial estate near Ashington was destroyed in a raging inferno that was visible for miles around. Occurring at just after 8.30 p.m., a total of fifteen pumps were needed before the fire was brought under control. Almost every fire engine in the county was mobilised, either in standby moves or to the fire itself, and reinforcements in the shape of two turntable ladders and four pumps were requested from Tyne and Wear Fire Brigade. Two further pumps were ordered to stand by at Cramlington and Blyth. It was a rare occasion that a turntable ladder was called to work in Northumberland and to date this is one of the few instances when two have operated simultaneously.

The busiest station in the brigade now was Blyth, which had turned out a total of 1,790 times during 1993. Of these, 333 were standbys at other stations. Ashington was the second busiest. The station attending the least amount of calls was Allendale, which turned out a total of thirty-five times.

Once again the New Year was dominated by continued budget cuts and the need to identify savings. In October 1992 Alnwick fire station was reduced from full-time and retained manning to fully retained, a major change from the day manning proposals. In June of the following year both Hexham and Berwick became day manned. The county council had at last achieved its objectives. These reductions in manning would result in savings of at least £170,000.

Cramlington's crew tackles a Ford Fiesta on fire on the A1 at Stannington. Car fires helped to boost the figures for fires in 1990.

Right: *Berwick crews were first to arrive when this rubber factory at Hadstone caught fire in March 1990. (Courtesy of* Newcastle Chronicle & Journal)

Below: *Only the outer walls remain of the Grey Arms Public House, Red Row, near Morpeth, after it was gutted by fire in November 1991. (Courtesy of* Newcastle Chronicle & Journal)

To meet the requirements of the standards of fire cover in the west of the county, a new satellite fire station was commissioned at Hexham, on the opposite side of the town to the main fire station. Not a very elaborate structure, the building was basically a corrugated steel affair big enough to house the retained water tender. Amble also finally got its new station. Although a suitable site had been procured long before, the lack of finance continually saw the construction deferred. The new station was opened in December and one appliance and the retained personnel were transferred to this site. Now the fire station replacement programme was complete. It had been a long struggle and had taken almost forty-four years.

New appliances to replace the aging Fords continued to be delivered. In 1993 six further Volvo water tenders were ordered, together with a series of trailers housing specialist equipment. One was a forward support unit trailer that could be utilised for forward communications, command and control, and as a rest, feeding or fuel supply area. Also part of the system were two lighting control units carrying sufficient portable halogen lights and telescopic masts to illuminate an area as large as a football field. These were based in the north and west of the county.

Two serious fires were reported at the beginning and end of 1993. In April Northumbria Bus Company's depot at Blyth suffered a severe fire that resulted in the total destruction of two double-decker buses and serious damage to surrounding vehicles. Firefighting was hampered by the close proximity of the parked buses, making access difficult for the fire crews. Appliances from Blyth, Cramlington and Ashington attended. Damage here was estimated at £500,000.

Fires at any time are always tragic events for someone, but those that occur at Christmas are even more so. In December two children's lives were lost in a three-storey terraced maisonette at Ashington. Four pumps were needed at this fire. Earlier on, in June, six people were killed in

The spacious new, hi-tech command and control centre, constructed in the former AFS garages at Morpeth, was a far cry from the rudimentary equipment that was in place at The Grove.

a single road accident on a single carriageway section of the A1 at Charlton Mires. Appliances from Alnwick and Belford were the unfortunate crews called by the ambulance service to assist at this horrific accident. The end of this year saw a 6 per cent decrease in the brigade's activity, partly put down to the poor summer and high rainfall. Calls totalled 4,993, of which 2,227 were fires. Chimney fires totalled 326 and there were a staggering 743 malicious calls. On a happier note Cramlington personnel won their way to the semi-finals in the Fire Services National Technical Competition, a first for the county.

Ten years after the second Morpeth train crash, yet another train was derailed in the same area. This accident occurred on 27 June 1993, just outside the railway station at Coopies Lane. On this occasion a northbound Royal Mail train was derailed and ploughed into the embankment, trapping the driver in his cab. In view of previous incidents at this location a predetermined attendance of six pumps was immediately mobilised. Upon arrival it was found that the only casualty was the locomotive driver who was rapidly extricated and transported to hospital.

In August the previous year the brigade had commissioned a new fire safety unit trailer for carrying the fire safety and prevention message out to schools and the general community. The unit was furnished with an assortment of audiovisual materials and an interactive CD system, and had a capacity of twenty-five pupils. In April the unit was officially launched at the International Fire Show at Hannover in Germany while, on 1 April, the new command and control complex went live. The complex, situated in the former AFS garages in the rear yard at Morpeth, was officially opened on 6 March 1994 by Councillor J.W. Whiteman, chairman of the Public Protection and General Purposes Committee. A secondary command and control complex was established at Amble fire station for use if the main centre ever needed to be evacuated.

Owing to improved methods of storage and increased fire prevention measures, the number of large farm fires had dwindled substantially, although they still occurred from time to time. September 1994 was no exception and the frustrating sight of tons of straw burning just after the harvest was always a tragic occasion for the farmer. On the night of the 20th, fire destroyed 250 tons of baled hay and straw and 1,200 tons of corn at Burnthouse Farm, Netherton, near Morpeth. Six pumps attended the fire and water had to be ferried from hydrants a mile away and from open water half a mile distant. The crews successfully stopped the fire spreading to fertilisers stored in the vicinity but remained on the scene throughout the night on damping down operations.

Interesting incidents for 1995 started with a large fire at Oliver's Paper Mill in Morpeth, where on the brigade's arrival, a raging fire was in progress on the upper three floors of the five-storey building. There was a great danger of the building collapsing while fire-fighting operations were in progress. Six of the brigade's pumps attended this fire.

In April the northwest of the county was the scene of another moorland fire, which resulted in 50 hectares of heather and 20 hectares of forest being destroyed. The fire originated at Linsheil, Otterburn, close to the villages of Harbottle and Holystone, and was of such ferocity that evacuation of the villages was considered at one time. Ten pumps were mobilised and with the assistance of 120 armed forces personnel from nearby Otterburn Camp, it was finally extinguished but not before large tracts of vegetation were destroyed. Appliances attended from stations at Bellingham, Rothbury, Morpeth, Hexham, Allendale, Haydon Bridge and Haltwhistle.

In July overheating mixing vessels at Pontin's dye works in Princess Way, Prudhoe, released large volumes of noxious red gas into the atmosphere. Public warnings had to be given to local residents to remain indoors while part of the area was cordoned off. Six firefighters in chemical protection suits and breathing apparatus made the area safe by neutralising the chemicals with caustic soda. Three Northumberland pumps and the chemical incident trailer supplemented by one appliance from Tyne and Wear were in attendance at this incident.

The standards of fire cover audit, on which so much time and effort had been spent during the preceding ten years, was still continuing. Having previously determined that the present locations of the south Northumberland fire stations made it difficult to meet the required attendance times to the village of Hollywell, a new fire station was opened in 1996 on the east side of Cramlington. The establishment was set at two full-time pumps, the second one being transferred from Blyth. The original Cramlington fire station, not yet twenty-five years old, was unceremoniously closed.

By this time the brigade had another chief fire officer. Jeff Ord had left in December to take up a position as chief fire officer of the South Yorkshire Metropolitan Fire Brigade. His replacement was John McCall from Grampian Fire Brigade. His fire service career began with the Western Area of Scotland Fire Brigade, progressing through the ranks in brigades in West Sussex, Kent, Grampian and Strathclyde. During his career he was involved in a number of major emergencies, notably the *Herald of Free Enterprise* ferry disaster at Zeebrugge, the Deal barracks bombing in which eleven Royal Marines lost their lives, and the great storms that devastated part of South East England in October 1987. After a lapse of some years, Northumberland's fire brigade was once again under the command of a man from north of the border. At the time of this appointment, the strength of the brigade was 203 full-time firefighters and 155 part-time staff.

It is interesting to record that during 1996 two fires were dealt with on Holy Island. The area was now adequately covered by crews from either Berwick or Belford, who were airlifted as and when required. There had been no further correspondence with the islanders about local cover; it looked as if the previously embittered discussions had been peacefully resolved.

With the major fires at Shiellaw Crags almost distant memories, Bellingham was turned out on the early evening of 10 April to Blackburn Common near Greenhaugh, where 200 acres of heath was blazing. Five additional pumps supplemented the Bellingham men in fighting this remote fire and, with the aid of beaters and main jets supplied from light portable pumps, prevented the fire from gaining any ground.

In April the second pump at Cramlington was transferred back to Blyth, reversing the 1994 move where it was thought that better 'global' fire cover could be provided. The vacant bay at Cramlington was occupied by a paramedic ambulance of the Northumbria Ambulance Service under the two authorities' co-location programme. This programme saw a number of Northumbria ambulance stations close or the relocation of ambulances into fire stations, at which staff would jointly share facilities. The arrangement was an economical proposition for the ambulance service and also provided additional income for the fire service. The first co-location had occurred at Blyth, when an ambulance from Ashington was transferred into the town, followed shortly after by similar arrangements at Cramlington when Seaton Deleval ambulance station was closed down. Later, similar schemes were developed at Amble, Prudhoe and Seahouses, although at the latter the arrangement was short-lived despite a new garage building being constructed to accommodate an ambulance.

To supplement the welcome income from the joint ambulance co-location, a more unusual way of earning income was devised. Fire engines were used as convenient advertising boards in the same way that public transport vehicles have traditionally been. By the end of 1997 the county's Volvo fire engines were all carrying legends on the side lockers advertising 'firefighters with Gore-tex protection'.

By the end of 1997 there were twenty-six Volvo water tenders in service. Most of the Fords had been auctioned off, but there were still three of the Dodge Commandos left in service. There would have been four but in September that year Morpeth's example overturned after spinning out of control while on its way to a road accident at Belsay. The accident on the Morpeth to Walton road left the appliance completely on its roof in a field, wrecked. Importantly though, the steel safety cab ensured that none of the five crew were seriously injured. The appliance was fifteen years old and was therefore written off, ending its days in a scrap yard at Lynemouth. Another of the Dodges was driven out to Bosnia by fire personnel under the auspices of the Fire-Aid programme that saw pensioned off fire appliances donated to underprivileged countries.

The busiest full-time fire station in Northumberland was still Blyth, with its two full-time manned appliances, while the busiest retained fire station was Prudhoe. The quietest station was Belford, which responded on fifty-three occasions. This year the brigade attended 5,102 incidents. Chimney fires totalled 255 and there were over 2,000 false alarms, of which 379 were malicious.

Approval was given in 1998 for the purchase of two bulk water carriers, which could also be used for driver training. This was later rescinded owing to financial constraints. Alnwick fire station, the first one to be completed under the brigade's early postwar renewal programme, was identified as being due for replacement in the near future and, although only thirty years old, the downgrading of the station to retained status meant that there was a surplus of space and accommodation, and renovation was to be expected in the future.

On 29 June 1998 Berwick Fire Brigade were called out to their biggest fire in several years. At 9 p.m. fire was reported at Shorts Mill on Dock Road at Tweedmouth, where it was discovered that the roof and top floors of the five-storey mill used as a food-processing and storage plant were spewing out angry red flames. Owing to the height of the building, a turntable ladder was immediately requested, the nearest one being with the Lothian and Borders Fire Brigade at Edinburgh, which was quickly mobilised for the long journey to Berwick. Owing to the seriousness of the fire a further five pumps, including two from over the border, were ordered to the fire, together with the brigade's incident command unit. Eight jets and a monitor from the Scottish turntable ladder appliance were quickly directing water into the building and after a strenuous two-hour battle the fire was brought under control. This was another one of the very rare occasions that a turntable ladder has been used in the county.

The year 1998 marked the fiftieth anniversary of Northumberland County as a fire authority. In this relatively short period, the brigade, starting with a motley assembly of prewar and wartime fire appliances operating mainly from requisitioned and temporary premises, had steadily developed into a fire and rescue service equipped with the latest that modern technology and funding allow. Under the initial command of the illustrious Chief Fire Officer William Bell Muir and the succeeding six chief officers, the brigade has overcome many major obstacles, such as the major reorganisation of 1974, which saw four busy fire stations transferred to another authority, and then the major fire cover review of the 1990s, which saw some fire stations downgraded in status. The county currently covers an area of over 2,000 square miles and contains all types of risks, from extensive forest and rural areas to densely populated urban areas with industrial risks in docks and chemical plants. Covering this area are nineteen fire stations, all dating from after the war and all equipped with the latest appliances constructed to standard specifications. These are manned by a highly trained workforce of firefighters, who are supported by a range of ancillary staff including officers, adinistrators, control room and administration staff, as well as workshop staff. All of the above, both past and present, have contributed in making Northumberland Fire & Rescue Service the highly efficient and respected brigade that it is today.

Other titles published by Tempus

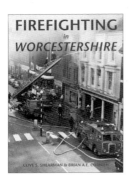

Firefighting in Worcestershire

CLIVE S. SHEARMAN & BRIAN A.E. CORNISH

After the Second World War the Fire Service we know and recognise today was formed. This book shows the impact of fire and firefighting in Worcestershire. Inside are images telling the story of firefighting in the county, showing the men, the engines and the fires, and other disasters they encountered.

07524-3166-8

Firefighting in Kent

ROGER MARDON & JOHN MEAKINS

This book traces the story of firefighting in Kent, and is complemented by over 200 photographs of fire engines, brigades, street scenes, and architecture. Roger Mardon has written two previous books about firefighting, and John Meakins is the curator of Kent Fire Brigade Museum. *Firefighting in Kent* is a must for fire service and vehicle enthusiasts, as well as local people and historians.

07524-3260-5

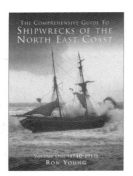

Shipwrecks of the North East Coast
Volume 1 (1740-1917)

RON YOUNG

In this comprehensive volume, Ron Young, an experienced diver, catalogues the histories of the ships that have been stranded and wrecked along the north-east coast of England, from Whitby to Berwick-upon-Tweed. He records the bravery of the lifeboat crews that have risked their lives to rescue the survivors.

07524-1749-5

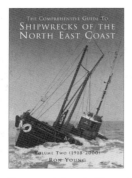

Shipwrecks of the North East Coast
Volume 2 (1918-2000)

RON YOUNG

In this second volume, Ron Young assesses the numerous wrecks as diving and boat angling sites, giving co-ordinates and dimensions, and describing the marine life and treasures to be found on the seabed along this busy and treacherous stretch of coastline.

07524-1750-9

If you are interested in purchasing other books published by Tempus, or in case you have difficulty finding any Tempus books in your local bookshop, you can also place orders directly through our website

www.tempus-publishing.com